JAMES RUSSELL LOWELL

From the crayon by S. W. Rowse in the possession of Professor Charles Eliot Norton

JAMES RUSSELL LOWELL
AND HIS FRIENDS.

BY

EDWARD EVERETT HALE

WITH PORTRAITS, FACSIMILES, AND OTHER
ILLUSTRATIONS

AMS PRESS
NEW YORK

Second AMS Printing 1969

Reprinted from a copy in the collections of
Northwestern University Library
From the edition of 1899, Cambridge
First AMS EDITION published 1965
Manufactured in the United States of America

Library of Congress Catalogue Card Number: 71-97165

AMS PRESS, INC.
New York, N.Y. 10003

CONTENTS

ILLUSTRATIONS

JAMES RUSSELL LOWELL
AND HIS FRIENDS

CHAPTER I

HIS BOYHOOD AND EARLY LIFE

ONE cannot conceive more fortunate or charming conditions than those of the boyhood and early education of James Russell Lowell. You may study the babyhood and boyhood of a hundred poets and not find one home like his. His father, the Rev. Charles Lowell, was the minister of a large parish in Boston for more than fifty years. Before James was born, Dr. Lowell had moved his residence from Boston to Cambridge, to the home which his children afterwards called Elmwood. So much of Mr. Lowell's poetry refers to this beautiful place, as beautiful now as it was then, that even far-away readers will feel a personal interest in it.

The house, not much changed in the last century, was one of the Cambridge houses deserted by the Tory refugees at the time of the Revolution. On the steps of this house Thomas Oliver, who lived there in 1774, stood and heard the demand of the freeholders of Middlesex County when they came to bid him resign George the Third's commission. The king had appointed him lieutenant-governor of Massachusetts and president of the council. But by the charter of the province councilors were to be elected. Thomas Oliver became, therefore, an object of public resentment. A committee of gentlemen of the county waited on him on the morning of September 2, 1774, at this house, not then called Elmwood. At their request he waited at once on General Gage in Boston, to prevent the coming of any troops out from town to meet the Middlesex yeomanry. And he was able to report to them in the afternoon that no troops had been ordered, "and, from the account I had given his Excellency, none would be ordered." The same afternoon, however, four or five thousand men appeared, not from the town but from the country — "a quarter part in arms." For in truth this was a rehearsal for the minute-men's gathering of the next spring, on the morning of the battle of Lexington. They insisted on Oliver's resignation of his commission from the crown, and he at last signed the resignation they had prepared, with this addition: "My house at Cambridge being surrounded by five thousand people, in compliance with their command, I sign my name."

But for Thomas Oliver's intercession with General Gage and the Admiral of the English fleet, the English troops would have marched to Cambridge that day, and Elmwood would have been the battle-ground of the First Encounter.

The state confiscated his house after Governor

Oliver left for England. Elbridge Gerry, one of the signers of the Declaration, occupied it afterward.

Readers must remember that in Cambridge were Washington's headquarters, and that the centre of the American army lay in Cambridge. During this time the large, airy rooms of Elmwood were used for the hospital service of the centre. Three or four acres of land belonged to the estate. Since those early days a shorter road than the old road from Watertown to Cambridge has been cut through on the south of the house, which stands, therefore, in the midst of a triangle of garden and meadow. But it was and is well screened from observation by high lilac hedges and by trees, mostly elms and pines. It is better worth while to say all this than it might be were we speaking of some other life, for, as the reader will see, the method of education which was followed out with James Russell Lowell and his brothers and sisters made a little world for them within the confines, not too narrow, of the garden and meadow of Elmwood.

In this home James Russell Lowell was born, on the 22d of February, 1819. There is more than one reference in his letters to his being born on Washington's birthday. His father, as has been said, was the Rev. Charles Lowell. His mother before her marriage was Harriet Spence, daughter of Mary Traill, who was the daughter of Robert Traill, of Orkney. They were of the same family to which Minna Troil, of Scott's novel of "The Pirate," belongs. Some of us like to think that the second-sight and the weird fancies without which a poet's

life is not fully rounded came to the child of Elmwood direct by the blood and traditions of Norna
and the Fitful Head. Anyway, Mrs. Lowell was a
person of remarkable nature and accomplishments.
In the very close of her life her health failed, from
difficulties brought on by the bad food and other
exposure of desert travel in the East with her husband. Those were the prehistoric days when travelers in Elijah's deserts did not carry with them a
cook from the Palais Royal. But such delicate
health was not a condition of the early days of the
poet's life.

His mother had the sense, the courage, and exquisite foresight which placed the little boy, almost
from his birth, under the personal charge of a sister
eight years older. Mrs. Putnam died on the 1st of
June, 1898, loving and beloved, after showing the
world in a thousand ways how well she was fitted
for the privileges and duties of the nurse, playmate,
companion, philosopher, and friend of a poet. She
entered into this charge, I do not know how early —
I suppose from his birth. I hope that we shall hear
that she left in such form that they may be printed
her notes on James's childhood and her care of it.

Certain general instructions were given by father
and mother, and under these the young Mentor was
largely left to her own genius and inspiration. A
daily element in the business was the little boy's
nap. He was to lie in his cradle for three hours
every morning. His little nurse, eleven or twelve
years old, might sing to him if she chose, but she
generally preferred to read to him from the poets

ENTRANCE TO ELMWOOD

who interested her. The cadences of verse were soothing, and so the little boy fell asleep every day quieted by the rhythm of Shakespeare or Spenser. By the time a boy is three years old he does not feel much like sleeping three hours in the forenoon. Also, by that time this little James began to be interested in the stories in Spenser, and Mrs. Putnam once gave me a most amusing account of the struggle of this little blue-eyed fellow to resist the coming of sleep and to preserve his consciousness so that he might not lose any of the poem.

Of course the older sister had to determine, in doubtful cases, whether this or that pastime or occupation conflicted with the general rules which had been laid down for them. In all the years of this tender intimacy they never had but one misunderstanding. He was quite clear that he had a right to do this; she was equally sure that he must do that. For a minute it seemed as if there were a parting of the ways. There was no assertion of authority on her part; there could be none. But he saw the dejection of sorrow on her face. And this was enough. He rushed back to her, yielded the whole point, and their one dispute was at an end. The story is worth telling, if only as an early and exquisite exhibition of the profound affection for others which is at the basis of Lowell's life. If to this loving-kindness you add an extraordinary self-control, you have the leading characteristics of his nature as it appears to those who knew him earliest and best, and who have such right to know where the motives of his life are to be found.

I am eager to go on in some reminiscences of the little Arcadia of Elmwood. But I must not do this till I have said something of the noble characteristics of the boy's father. Indeed, I must speak of the blood which was in the veins of father and son, that readers at a distance from Boston may be reminded of a certain responsibility which attaches in Massachusetts to any one who bears the Lowell name.

I will go back only four generations, when the Rev. John Lowell was the Congregational minister of Newburyport, and so became a leader of opinion in Essex County. This man's son, James Lowell's grandfather, the second John Lowell, is the Lowell who as early as 1772 satisfied himself that, at the common law, slavery could not stand in Massachusetts. It is believed that he offered to a negro, while Massachusetts was still a province of the Crown, to try if the courts could not be made to liberate him as entitled to the rights of Englishmen. This motion of his may have been suggested by Lord Mansfield's decision in 1772, in the Somerset case, which determined, from that day to this day, that —

> " Slaves cannot breathe in England ; if their lungs
> Receive our air, that moment they are free !
> They touch our country, and their shackles fall ! "

But in that year John Lowell lost his chance. In 1779, however, he introduced the clause in our Massachusetts Bill of Rights under which the Supreme Court of Massachusetts freed every slave in the state who sought his freedom. Let me say in passing that some verses of his, written when he was quite a young man, are preserved in the "Pietas et Gratulatio." This was an elegant volume which Harvard College prepared and sent to George III. in 1760 on his accession to the crown. They are written with the exaggeration of a young man's verse; but they show, not only that he had the ear for rhythm and something of what I call the "lyric swing," but also that he had the rare art of putting things. There is snap and epigram in the lines. Here they differ by the whole sky from the verses of James Russell, who was also a great-grandfather of our poet Lowell. This gentleman, a resident of Charlestown, printed a volume of poems, which is now very rare. I am, very probably, the only person in the world who has ever read it, and I can testify that there is not one line in the book which is worth remembering, if, indeed, any one could remember a line of it.

John Lowell, the emancipator, became a judge. He had three sons, — John Lowell, who, without office, for many years led Massachusetts in her political trials; Francis Cabot Lowell, the founder of the city of Lowell; and Charles Lowell, the father of the poet. It is Francis Lowell's son who founded the Lowell Institute, the great popular university of Boston. It is Judge John Lowell's grandson who directs that institution with wonderful wisdom; and it is his son who gives us from day to day the last intelligence about the crops in Mars, or reverses the opinions of centuries as to the daily duties of Mercury and Venus. I say all this by way of illustration as to what we have a right to expect of a

Lowell, and, if you please, of what James Russell Lowell demanded of himself as soon as he knew what blood ran in his veins.

In this connection one thing must be said with a certain emphasis; for the impression has been given that James Russell Lowell took up his anti-slavery sentiment from lessons which he learned from the outside after he left college.

The truth is that Wilberforce's portrait hung opposite his father's face in the dining-room. And it was not likely that in that house people had forgotten who wrote the anti-slavery clauses in the Massachusetts Bill of Rights only forty years before Lowell was born.

Before he was a year old the Missouri Compromise passed Congress. The only outburst of rage remembered in that household was when Charles Lowell, the father, lost his self-control, on the morning when he read his newspaper announcing that capitulation of the North to its Southern masters. It took more than forty years before that same household had to send its noblest offering to the war which should undo that capitulation. It was forty-five years before Lowell delivered the Harvard Commemoration Ode under the college elms.

We are permitted to publish for the first time a beautiful portrait of the Rev. Charles Lowell when he was at his prime. The picture does more than I can do to give an impression of what manner of man he was, and to account for the regard, which amounts to reverence, with which people who knew him speak of him to this hour. The reader at a

REV. CHARLES LOWELL

From a painting in the possession of Charles Lowell, Boston

distance must try to imagine what we mean when we speak of a Congregational minister in New England at the end of the last century and at the beginning of this. We mean a man who had been chosen by a congregation of men to be their spiritual teacher for his life through, and, at the same time, the director of sundry important functions in the administration of public affairs. When one speaks of the choice of Charles Lowell to be a minister in Boston, it is meant that the selection was made by men who were his seniors, perhaps twice his age, among whom were statesmen, men of science, leaders at the bar, and merchants whose sails whitened all the ocean. Such men made the selection of their minister from the young men best educated, from the most distinguished families of the State.

In 1805 Charles Lowell returned from professional study in Edinburgh. He had been traveling that summer with Mr. John Lowell, his oldest brother. In London he had seen Wilberforce, who introduced him into the House of Commons, where he heard Fox and Sheridan. Soon after he arrived in Boston he was invited to preach at the West Church.

This church was the church of Mayhew, who was the Theodore Parker of his time. Mayhew was in the advance in the Revolutionary sentiment of his day, and Samuel Adams gave to him the credit of having first suggested the federation of the Colonies: " Adams, we have a communion of churches; why do we not make a communion of states?" This he said after leaving the communion table.

In such a parish young Charles Lowell preached in 1805, from the text, "Rejoice in the Lord alway." Soon after, he was unanimously invited to settle as its minister, and in that important charge he remained until he died, on the 20th of January, 1861.

Mr. Lowell was always one of those who interpreted most broadly and liberally the history and principles of the Christian religion. But he was never willing to join in the unfortunate schism which divided the Congregational churches between Orthodox and Unitarian. He and Dr. John Pierce, of Brookline, to their very death, succeeded in maintaining a certain nominal connection with the Evangelical part of the Congregational body.

The following note, written thirty-six years after James Lowell was born, describes his position in the disputes of " denominationalists " : —

MY DEAR SIR : You must allow me to say that, whilst I am most happy to have my name announced as a contributor toward any fund that may aid in securing freedom and religious instruction to Kansas, I do not consent to its being announced as the minister of a Unitarian or Trinitarian church, in the common acceptation of those terms. If there is anything which I have uniformly, distinctly, and emphatically declared, it is that I have adopted no other religious creed than the Bible, and no other name than Christian as denoting my religious faith.

Very affectionately your friend and brother,

CHA. LOWELL.

ELMWOOD, CAMBRIDGE,
    December 19, 1855.

It may be said that he was more known as a minister than as a preacher. There was no branch of ministerial duty in which he did not practically engage. His relations with his people, from the beginning to the end, were those of entire confidence. But it must be understood, while this is said, that he was a highly popular preacher everywhere, and every congregation, as well as that of the West Church, was glad if by any accident of courtesy or of duty he appeared in the pulpit.

The interesting and amusing life by which the children of the family made a world of the gardens of Elmwood was in itself an education. The garden and grounds, as measured by a surveyor, were only a few acres. But for a circle of imaginative children, as well led as the Lowell children were, this is a little world. One is reminded of that fine passage in Miss Trimmers's "Robins," where, when the four little birds have made their first flight from the nest into the orchard, Pecksy says: "Mamma, what a large place the world is!" Practically, I think, for the earlier years of James Lowell's life, Elmwood furnished as large a world as he wanted. Within its hedges and fences the young people might do much what they chose. They were Mary, who was the guardian; then came William; afterwards Robert, whose name is well known in our literature; and then James. The four children were much together; they found nothing difficult, for work or for pastime. Another daughter, Rebecca, was the songstress of the home; with a sweet flexible voice she sang, in her childhood, hymns, and afterwards the Scotch melodies and the other popular music of the day.

The different parts of the grounds of Elmwood became to these children different cities of the world, and they made journeys from one to another. Their elder brother Charles, until he went to Exeter to school, joined in this geographical play.

The father and mother differed from each other, but were allied in essentials; they enjoyed the same tastes and followed the same pursuits in literature and art.   Dr. Lowell was intimate with Allston, the artist, whose studio was not far away, and the progress of his work was a matter of home conversation.

Mrs. Putnam told me that in " The First Snowfall " would be found a reference to Lowell's elder brother William, who died when the poet himself was but five years old; another trace of this early memory appears again in the poem " Music," in " A Year's Life."

To such open-air life we may refer the pleasure he always took in the study of birds, their seasons and habits, and the accuracy of his knowledge with regard to trees and wild flowers.

In the simple customs of those days, when one clergyman exchanged pulpits with another, Dr. Lowell would drive in his own " chaise " to the parsonage of his friend, would spend the day there, and return probably on Monday morning.   He soon found that James was a good companion in such rides, and the little fellow had many reminiscences of these early travels.   It would be easy to quote

THE PASTURE, ELMWOOD

hundreds of references in his poems and essays to
the simple Cambridge life of these days before college. Thus here are some lines from the poem
hardly known, on " The Power of Music."

> " When, with feuds like Ghibelline and Guelf,
>   Each parish did its music for itself,
>   A parson's son, through tree-arched country ways,
>   I rode exchanges oft in dear old days,
>   Ere yet the boys forgot, with reverent eye,
>   To doff their hats as the black coat went by,
>   Ere skirts expanding in their apogee
>   Turned girls to bells without the second e ;
>   Still in my teens, I felt the varied woes
>   Of volunteers, each singing as he chose,
>   Till much experience left me no desire
>   To learn new species of the village choir."

So soon as the boy was old enough he was sent
to the school of Mr. William Wells, an English
gentleman who kept a classical school in Cambridge,
not far from Dr. Lowell's house. Of this school Dr.
Holmes and Mr. Higginson have printed some of
their memories. All the Cambridge boys who were
going to college were sent there. Mr. Wells was a
good Latin scholar, and on the shelves of old-fashioned men will still be found his edition of Tacitus,
printed under his own eye in Cambridge, and one
of the tokens of that " Renaissance " in which Cambridge and Boston meant to show that they could
push such things with as much vigor and success as
they showed in the fur trade or in privateering. A
very good piece of scholarly work it is. Mr. Wells
was a well-trained Latinist from the English schools,
and his boys learned their Latin well. And it is
worth the while of young people to observe that in

the group of men of letters at Cambridge and Boston, before and after James Lowell's time, Samuel Eliot, William Orne White, James Freeman Clarke, Charles and James Lowell, John and Wendell Holmes, Charles Sumner, Wentworth Higginson, and other such men never speak with contempt of the niceties of classical scholarship. You would not catch one of them in a bad quantity, as you sometimes do catch to-day even a college president, if you are away from Cambridge, in the mechanical Latin of his Commencement duty.

But though the boys might become good Latinists and good Grecians, the school has not a savory memory as to the personal relations between master and pupils. James Lowell, however, knew but little of its hardships, as he was but a day scholar. Dr. Samuel Eliot, who attended the school as a little boy, tells me that Lowell delighted to tell the boys imaginative tales, and the little fellows, or many of them, took pleasure in listening to the more stirring stories. " I remember nothing of them except one, which rejoiced in the central interest of a trap in the playground, which opened to subterranean marvels of various kinds."

CHAPTER II

HARVARD COLLEGE

FROM such life, quite familiar with Cambridge and its interests, Lowell presented himself for entrance at Harvard College in the summer of 1834, and readily passed the somewhat strict examination which was required.

Remember, if you please, or learn now, if you never knew, that "Harvard College" was a college by itself, or "seminary," as President Quincy used to call it, and had no vital connection with the law school, the school of medicine, or the divinity school, — though they were governed by the same Board of Fellows, and, with the college, made up Harvard University. Harvard College was made of four classes, — numbering, all told, some two hundred and fifty young men, of all ages from fourteen to thirty-five. Most of them were between sixteen and twenty-two. In this college they studied Latin, Greek, and mathematics chiefly. But on " modern language days," which were Monday, Wednesday, and Friday, there appeared teachers of French, Italian, Spanish, German, and Portuguese; and everybody not a freshman must take his choice in these studies. They were called " voluntaries," not because you could shirk if you wanted to, for you could not, but because you chose German or Italian or Spanish or French or Portuguese. When you had once chosen, you had to keep on for four terms. But as to college "marks" and the rank which followed, a modern language was "worth" only half a classical language.

Beside these studies, as you advanced you read more or less in rhetoric, logic, moral philosophy, political economy, chemistry, and natural history, — less rather than more. There was no study whatever of English literature, but the best possible drill in the writing of the English language. There was a well selected library of about fifty thousand volumes, into which you might go on any week-day at any time before four o'clock and read anything you wanted. You took down the book with your own red right hand, and you put it back when you were done.

Then there were three or four society libraries. To these you contributed an entrance fee, when you were chosen a member, and an annual fee of perhaps two dollars. With this money the society bought almost all the current novels of the time. Novels were then published in America in two volumes, and they cost more than any individual student liked to pay. One great object in joining a college society was to have a steady supply of novels. For my part, I undoubtedly averaged eighty novels a year in my college course. They were much better novels, in my judgment, than the average novels of to-day are, and I know I received great advantage from the time I devoted to reading them. I think

Lowell would have said the same thing. But I do not mean to imply that such reading was his principal reading. He very soon began delving in the stores which the college library afforded him of the older literature of England.

You had to attend morning chapel and evening chapel. Half the year these offices were at six in the morning and six at night. But as the days shortened, morning prayers came later and later, — even as late as half past seven in the morning, — while afternoon prayers came as early as quarter past four, so that the chapel need not be artificially lighted. On this it followed that breakfast, which was an hour and twenty minutes after prayers, might be long after eight in the morning, and supper at half past four in the afternoon. This left enormously long evenings for winter reading.

Lowell found in the government some interesting and remarkable men.

Josiah Quincy, the president, had been the mayor of Boston who had to do with ordering the system and precedents of its government under the new city charter. From a New England town, governed by the fierce democracy of town meetings, he changed it into a " city," as America calls it, ruled by an intricate system of mayor, aldermen, council, school committee, and overseers of the poor. Of a distinguished patriot family, Mr. Quincy had been, for years of gallant battle, a leader in Congress of the defeated and disconcerted wrecks of the Federal party. His white plume never went down, and he fought the Southern oligarchy as cheerfully as

Amadis ever fought with his uncounted enemies. He was old enough to have been an aide to Governor Hancock when Washington visited Boston in 1792. In Congress he had defied John Randolph, who was an antagonist worthy of him; and he hated Jefferson, and despised him, I think, with a happy union of scorn and hatred, till he died. When he was more than ninety, after the civil war began, I had my last interview with him. He was rejoiced that the boil had at last suppurated and was ready to be lanced, and that the thing was to be settled in the right way. He said: " Gouverneur Morris once said to me that we made our mistake when we began, when we united eight republics with five oligarchies."

It is interesting now to know, what I did not know till after his death, that this gallant leader of men believed that he was directed, in important crises, by his own " Daimon," quite as Socrates believed. In the choice of his wife, which proved indeed to have been made in heaven, he knew he was so led. And, in after life, he ascribed some measures of importance and success to his prompt obedience to the wise Daimon's directions.

His wife was most amiable in her kind interest in the students' lives. The daughters who resided with him were favorites in the social circles of Cambridge.

Most of the work of the college was then done in rather dreary recitations, such as you might expect in a somewhat mechanical school for boys to-day. But Edward Tyrrel Channing, brother of

EDWARD TYRREL CHANNING

the great divine, met his pupils face to face and hand to hand. He deserves the credit of the English of Emerson, Holmes, Sumner, Clarke, Bellows, Lowell, Higginson, and other men whom he trained. Their English did more credit to Harvard College, I think, than any other of its achievements for those thirty-two years. You sat, physically, at his side. He read your theme aloud with you, — so loud, if he pleased, that all of the class who were present could hear his remarks of praise or ridicule, — " Yes, we used to have white paper and black ink; now we have blue paper, blue ink." I wonder if Mr. Emerson did not get from him the oracle, " Leave out the adjectives, and let the nouns do the fighting." I think that is Emerson's. Or whose is it?

In 1836, when Lowell was a sophomore, Mr. Longfellow came to Cambridge, a young man, to begin his long and valuable life in the college. His presence there proved a benediction, and, I might say, marks an epoch in the history of Harvard. In the first place, he was fresh from Europe, and he gave the best possible stimulus to the budding interest in German literature. In the second place, he came from Bowdoin College, and in those days it was a very good thing for a Harvard undergraduate to know that there were people not bred in Cambridge quite as well read, as intelligent, as elegant and accomplished as any Harvard graduate. In the third place, Longfellow, though he was so young, ranked already distinctly as a man of letters. This was no broken-winded minister who had been made professor. He was not a lawyer without clients, or a doctor without patients, for whom "a place" had to be found. He was already known as a poet by all educated people in America. The boys had read in their "First Class Book" his "Summer Shower" verses. By literature, pure and simple, and the work of literature, he had won his way to the chair of the Smith professorship of modern literature, to which Mr. George Ticknor had already given distinction. Every undergraduate knew all this, and felt that young Longfellow's presence was a new feather in our cap, as one did not feel when one of our own seniors was made a tutor, or one of our own tutors was made a professor.

But, better than this for the college, Longfellow succeeded, as no other man did, in breaking that line of belt ice which parted the students from their teachers. Partly, perhaps, because he was so young; partly because he was agreeable and charming; partly because he had the manners of a man of the world, because he had spoken French in Paris and Italian in Florence; but chief of all because he chose, he was companion and friend of the undergraduates. He would talk with them and walk with them; would sit with them and smoke with them. You played whist with him if you met him of an evening. You never spoke contemptuously of him, and he never patronized you.

Lowell intimates, however, in some of his letters, that he had no close companionship with Longfellow in those boyish days. He shared, of course, as every one could, in the little Renaissance, if one may call it so, of interest in modern Continental literature, on Longfellow's arrival in Cambridge.

I cannot remember — I wish I could — whether it were Longfellow or Emerson who introduced Tennyson in college. That first little, thin volume of Tennyson's poems, with " Airy, fairy Lillian " and the rest, was printed in London in 1830. It was not at once reprinted in America. It was Emerson's copy which somebody borrowed in Cambridge and which we passed reverently from hand to hand.[1] Everybody who had any sense knew that a great poet had been born as well as we know it now. And it is always pleasant to me to remember that those first poems of his were handed about in manuscript as a new ode of Horace might have been handed round among the young gentlemen of Rome.

Carlyle's books were reprinted in America, thanks to Emerson, as fast as they were written. Lowell read them attentively, and the traces of Carlyle study are to be found in all Lowell's life, as in the life of all well educated Americans of his time.

I have written what I have of Channing and Longfellow with the feeling that Lowell would himself have said much more of the good which they did to all of us. I do not know how much his clear, simple, unaffected English style owes to Channing, but I am quite sure that he would have spoken most gratefully of his teacher.

Now as to the atmosphere of the college itself.

[1] That copy is still preserved, — among the treasures of Mr. Emerson's library in Concord, — beautifully bound, for such was his habit with books which he specially loved.

I write these words in the same weeks in which I am reading the life of Jowett at Oxford. It is curious, it is pathetic, to compare Balliol College in 1836-7 with Harvard College at the same time. So clear is it that the impulse and direction were given in Oxford by the teachers, while with us the impulse and direction were given by the boys. The boys invariably called themselves "men," even when they were, as Lowell was when he entered, but fifteen years old.

Let it be remembered, then, that the whole drift of fashion, occupation, and habit among the undergraduates ran in lines suggested by literature. Athletics and sociology are, I suppose, now the fashion at Cambridge. But literature was the fashion then. In November, when the state election came round, there would be the least possible spasm of political interest, but you might really say that nobody cared for politics. Not five "men" in college saw a daily newspaper. My classmate, William Francis Channing, would have been spoken of, I think, as the only Abolitionist in college in 1838, the year when Lowell graduated. I remember that Dr. Walter Channing, the brother of our professor, came out to lecture one day on temperance. There was a decent attendance of the undergraduates, but it was an attendance of pure condescension on their part.

Literature was, as I said, the fashion. The books which the fellows took out of the library, the books which they bought for their own subscription libraries, were not books of science, nor history, nor sociology, nor politics; they were books of literature. Some Philadelphia publisher had printed in one volume Coleridge's poems, Shelley's, and Keats's — a queer enough combination, but for its chronological fitness. And you saw this book pretty much everywhere. At this hour you will find men of seventy who can quote their Shelley as the youngsters of to-day cannot quote, shall I say, their Swinburne, their Watson, or their Walt Whitman. In the way of what is now called science (we then spoke of the moral sciences also) Daniel Treadwell read once a year some interesting technological lectures. The Natural History Society founded itself while Lowell was in college; but there was no general interest in science, except so far as it came in by way of the pure mathematics.

In the year 1840 I was at West Point for the first time, with William Story, Lowell's classmate and friend, and with Story's sister and mine. We enjoyed to the full the matchless hospitality of West Point, seeing its lions under the special care of two young officers of our own age. They had just finished their course, as we had recently finished ours at Harvard. One day when Story and I were by ourselves, after we had been talking of our studies with these gentlemen, Story said to me: "Ned, it is all very well to keep a stiff upper lip with these fellows, but how did you dare tell them that we studied about projectiles at Cambridge?"

"Because we did," said I.

"Did I ever study projectiles?" asked Story, puzzled.

"Certainly you did," said I. "You used to go up to Peirce Tuesday and Thursday afternoons in the summer when you were a junior, with a blue book which had a white back."

"I know I did," said Story; "and was I studying projectiles then? This is the first time I ever heard of it."

And I tell that story because it illustrates well enough the divorce between theory and fact which is possible in education. I do not tell it by way of blaming Professor Peirce or Harvard College. Story was not to be an artilleryman, nor were any of the rest of us, so far as we knew. Anyway, the choice of our specialty in life was to be kept as far distant as was possible.

CHAPTER III

"HARVARDIANA," a college magazine which ran for four years, belongs exactly to the period of Lowell's college life. Looking over it now, it seems to me like all the rest of them. That is, it is as good as the best and as bad as the worst.

There is not any great range for such magazines. The articles have to be short. And the writers know very little of life. All the same, a college magazine gives excellent training. Lowell was one editor of the fourth volume of "Harvardiana." I suppose he then read proof for the first time, and in a small way it introduced him into the life of an editor, — a life in which he afterwards did a great deal of hard work, which he did extremely well, as we shall presently see.

The editorial board of the year before, from whose hands the five editors of the class of '38 took "Harvardiana," was a very interesting circle of young men. They were, by the way, classmates and friends of Thoreau, who lived to be better known than they; but I think he was not of the editorial committee. The magazine was really edited in that year entirely by Charles Hayward, Samuel Tenney Hildreth, and Charles Stearns Wheeler. Horatio Hale, the philo-

logist, was in the same class and belonged to the
same set. He was named as one of the editors.
But he was appointed to Wilkes's exploring expedi-
tion a year before he graduated, — a remarkable
testimony, this, to his early ability in the lines of
study in which he won such distinction afterwards.
It is interesting and amusing to observe that his
first printed work was a vocabulary of the language
of some Micmac Indians, who camped upon the college grounds in the summer of 1834. Hale learned
the language from them, made a vocabulary, and
then set up the type and printed the book with his
own hand. Hayward, Hildreth, and Wheeler, who
carried on the magazine for its third volume, all
died young, before the age of thirty. Hayward had
written one or more of the lives in Sparks's "American Biography," Wheeler had distinguished himself
as a Greek scholar here and in Europe, and Hildreth,
as a young poet, had given promise for what we all
supposed was to be a remarkable future.

To this little circle somebody addressed himself
who wanted to establish a chapter of Alpha Delta
Phi in Cambridge in 1836. Who this somebody
was, I do not know. I wish I did. But he came
to Cambridge and met these leaders of the literary
work of the classes of '37 and '38, and among them
they agreed on the charter members for the forma-
tion of the Alpha Delta Phi chapter at Harvard.
The list of the members of the Harvard classes of
1837 and 1838 shows that these youngsters knew
already who their men of letters were. It consists of
fourteen names: John Bacon, John Fenwick Eustis,

Horatio Hale, Charles Hayward, Samuel Tenney Hildreth, Charles Stearns Wheeler, Henry Williams, James Ivers Trecothick Coolidge, Henry Lawrence Eustis, Nathan Hale, Rufus King, George Warren Lippitt, James Russell Lowell, and Charles Woodman Scates.

This is no place for a history of Alpha Delta Phi. At the moment when the Phi Beta Kappa fraternity, the oldest of the confederated college societies, gave up its secrets, Alpha Delta Phi was formed in Hamilton College of New York. I shall violate none of her secrets if I say, what the history of literature in America shows, that, in the earlier days at least, interest in literature was considered by those who directed the society as a very important condition in the selection of its members.

At Cambridge, when Lowell became one of its first members, there was a special charm in membership. Such societies were absolutely forbidden by a hard and fast rule. They must not be in Harvard College. The existence of the Alpha Delta chapter, therefore, was not to be known, even to the great body of the undergraduates. It had no public exercises. There was no public intimation of meetings. In truth, if its existence had been known, everybody connected with it would have been severely punished, under the college code of that day.

This element of secrecy gave, of course, a special charm to membership. I ought to say that, after sixty years, it makes it more difficult to write of its history. I was myself a member in '37, '38, and '39. Yet, in a somewhat full private diary which I

kept in those days, I do not find one reference to
my attendance at any meeting; so great was the
peril, to my boyish imagination, lest the myrmidons
of the "Faculty" should seize upon my papers and
examine them, and should learn from them any fact
regarding the history of this secret society.

But now, after sixty years, I will risk the ven-
geance of the authorities of the university. Perhaps
they will take away all our degrees, honorary and
otherwise; but we will venture. This very secret
society, after it was well at work, may have counted
at once twenty members, — seniors, juniors, and
sophomores. They clubbed their scanty means and
hired a small student's room in what is now Holyoke
Street, put in a table and stove and some chairs,
and subscribed for the English quarterlies and Blackwood. This room was very near the elegant and
convenient club-house owned by the society to-day,
if indeed this do not occupy the same ground, as I
think it does. Everybody had a pass-key. It was
thus a place where you could loaf and be quiet and
read, and where once a week we held our literary
meetings. Of other meetings, the obligations of
secrecy do not permit me to speak. One of my
friends, the other day, said that his earliest recollec-
tion of Lowell was finding him alone in this modest
club-room reading some article in an English review.
What happened was that we all took much more
interest in the work which the Alpha Delta provided
for us than we did in most of the work required of
us by the college.

At that time the conventional division of classes

at Cambridge made very hard and fast distinctions
between students of different classes.   Alpha Delta
broke up all this and brought us together as gentlemen ; and, naturally, the younger fellows did their
very best when they were to read in the presence
of their seniors.   I think, though I am not certain,
that I heard Lowell read there the first draft of his
papers on Old English Dramatists, which he published afterwards in my brother's magazine, the
" Boston Miscellany," and which were the subject
of the last course of lectures which he delivered.

From this little group of Alpha Delta men were
selected the editors of " Harvardiana " for 1837–38.
I suppose, indeed, that in some informal way Alpha
Delta chose them.   They were Rufus King, afterwards a leader of the bar in Ohio ; George Warren
Lippitt, so long our secretary of legation at Vienna ; Charles Woodman Scates, who went into the
practice of law in Carolina ; James Russell Lowell ;
and my brother, Nathan Hale, Jr.   All of them
stood, when chosen, in what we call the first half of
the class.   This meant that they were within the
number of twenty-four students who had had honors
at the several exhibitions up to that time.   In point
of fact, twenty-four was not half the class.   But
that phrase long existed ; I do not know how long.
Practically, to say of a graduate that he was in " the
first half of his class " meant that at these exhibitions, or at Commencement, he had received some
college honor.

I rather think that the average senior of that
year approved this selection of editors, and he

would have said in a general way that King and
Lippitt were expected to do that heavy work of
long eight-page articles which is supposed by boys
to make such magazines respected among the graduates; that Scates was relied upon for critical work;
that my brother was supposed to have inherited a
faculty for editing, and that on him and Lowell, in
the general verdict of the class, was imposed the
privilege of furnishing the poetry for the magazine
and making it entertaining. Of course it was expected that their year's "Harvardiana" would be
better than those of any before.

The five editors had the further privilege of assuming the whole pecuniary responsibility for the
undertaking. How this came out I do not know;
perhaps I never did. I do not think they ever
printed three hundred copies. I do not think they
ever had two hundred and fifty subscribers. The
volume contains the earliest of Lowell's printed
poems, some of which have never been reprinted,
and a copy is regarded by collectors as one of the
exceptionally rare nuggets in our literary history.

When this choice of editors was made, I lived
with my brother in Stoughton 22. In September,
at the time when the first number was published, we
had moved to Massachusetts 27, where I lived for
two years. Lowell had always been intimate in our
room, and from this time until the next March he
was there once or twice a day. Indeed, it was a
good editor's room, — we called it the best room
in college; and all of them made it their headquarters.

Unfortunately for my readers, the daguerreotype and photograph had not even begun in their benevolent and beneficent career. It was in the next year that Daguerre, in Paris, first exhibited his pictures. The French government rewarded him for his great discovery and published his process to the world. His announcements compelled Mr. Talbot, in England, to make public his processes on paper, which were the beginning of what we now call photography. I think my classmate, Samuel Longfellow, and I took from the window of this same room, Massachusetts 27, the first photograph which was taken in New England. It was made by a little camera intended for draughtsmen. The picture was of Harvard Hall, opposite. And the first portrait taken in Massachusetts was the copy in this picture of a bust of Apollo standing in the window of the college library, in Harvard Hall.

The daguerreotype was announced by Daguerre in January, 1839. He thus forced W. H. Fox Talbot's hand, and he read his paper on photographic drawings on January 31 of that year. This paper was at once published, and Longfellow and I worked from its suggestions.

Rufus King afterwards won for himself distinction and respect as a lawyer of eminence in Cincinnati. He was the grandson of the great Rufus King, the natural leader of the Federalists and of the North in the dark period of the reign of the House of Virginia. Our Rufus King's mother was the daughter of Governor Worthington, of Ohio. King had begun his early education at Kenyon

College, but came to Cambridge to complete his undergraduate course, and remained there in the law school under Story and Greenleaf. He then returned to Cincinnati, where he lived in distinguished practice in his profession until his death in 1891. "His junior partners were many of them men in the first rank of political, judicial, and professional eminence. But he himself steadily declined all political or even judicial trusts until, in 1874, he became a member of the Constitutional Convention of Ohio. Over this body he presided. He did not shrink from any work in education. He was active in the public schools. He was the chief workman in creating the Cincinnati Public Library, and, as one of the trustees of the McMicken bequest, he nursed it into the foundation of the University of Cincinnati. In 1875 he became Dean of the Faculty of the Law School, and served in that office for five years. Until his death he continued his lectures on Constitutional Law and the Law of Real Property. No citizen of Cincinnati was more useful or more honored."

Lowell was with Mr. King in the Cambridge law school.

Of the five editors, four became lawyers — so far, at least, as to take the degree of Bachelor of Laws at Cambridge. The fifth, George Warren Lippitt, from Rhode Island, remained in Cambridge after he graduated and studied at the divinity school.

There were other clergymen in his class, who attained, as they deserved, distinction afterwards. Lowell frequently refers in his correspondence to Coolidge, Ellis, Renouf, and Washburn. Lippitt's

articles in "Harvardiana" show more maturity, perhaps, than those of any of the others. He had
entered the class as a sophomore, and was the oldest, I believe, of the five. For ten years, from 1842
to 1852, he was a valuable preacher in the Unitarian church, quite unconventional, courageous, can-
did, and outspoken. He was without a trace of that
ecclesiasticism, which the New Testament writers
would call accursed, which is the greatest enemy of
Christianity to-day, and does more to hinder it than
any other device of Satan. In 1852 Lippitt sought
and accepted an appointment as secretary of legation to Vienna. He married an Austrian lady, and
represented the United States at the imperial court
there in one and another capacity for the greater
part of the rest of his life. He died there in 1891.

Charles Woodman Scates, also, like King and
Lippitt, entered the class after the freshman year.
There was a tender regard between him and Lowell.
When they graduated, Scates went to South Carolina to study law. But for his delicate health, I
think his name would be as widely known in the
Southern states as Rufus King's is in the valley of
the Ohio. I count it as a great misfortune that
almost all of Lowell's letters to him, in an intimate
and serious correspondence which covered many
years, were lost when the house in Germantown was
burned where he spent the last part of his life.
Fortunately, however, Mr. Norton had made considerable extracts from them in the volume of
Lowell's published letters. From one of these
letters which has been preserved, I copy a little

poem, which I believe has never been printed.
Lowell writes : —

"I will copy you a midnight improvisation, which
must be judged kindly accordingly. It is a mere
direct transcript of *actual* feelings, and *so far*
good : —

> " What is there in the midnight breeze
>   That tells of things gone by ?
> Why does the murmur of the trees
>   Bring tears into my eye ?
> O Night ! my heart doth pant for thee,
> Thy stars are lights of memory !
>
> " What is there in the setting moon
>   Behind yon gloomy pine,
> That bringeth back the broad high noon
>   Of hopes that once were mine ?
> Seemeth my heart like that pale flower
> That opes not till the midnight hour.
>
> " The day may make the eyes run o'er
>   From hearts that laden be,
> The sunset doth a music pour
>   Round rock and hill and tree ;
> But in the night wind's mournful blast
> There cometh somewhat of the Past.
>
> " In garish day I often feel
>   The Present's full excess,
> And o'er my outer soul doth steal
>   A deep life-weariness.
> But the great thoughts that midnight brings
> Look calmly down on earthly things.
>
> " Oh, who may know the spell that lies
>   In a few bygone years !
> These lines may one day fill my eyes
>   With Memory's doubtful tears—
> Tears which we know not if they be
> Of happiness or agony.

> " Open thy melancholy eyes,
>   O Night ! and gaze on me !
> That I may feel the charm that lies
>   In their dim mystery.
> Unveil thine eyes so gloomy bright
> And look upon my soul, O Night ! "

" Have you ever felt this ?   I have, many and many a time."

Of my dear brother, Nathan Hale, Jr., I will not permit myself to speak at any length. We shall meet him once and again as our sketch of Lowell's life goes on. It is enough for our purpose now that, though he prepared himself carefully for the bar, and, as a young man, opened a lawyer's office, the most of his life, until he died in 1872, was spent in the work of an editor. Our father had been an editor from 1809, and of all his children, boys and girls, it might be said that they were cradled in the sheets of a newspaper.

My brother was the editor of the Boston " Miscellany " in 1841, where Lowell and Story of their class were his chief coöperators. From that time forward he served the Boston " Advertiser," frequently as its chief; and when he died, he was one of the editors of " Old and New," his admirable literary taste and his delicate judgment presiding over that discrimination, so terrible to magazine editors, in the accepting or rejecting of the work of contributors.

All of these five boys, or young men, were favorite pupils of Professor Edward Tyrrell Channing. When, in September, 1837, they undertook the publication of " Harvardiana," Lowell was eighteen,

Hale was eighteen, Scates, King, and Lippitt but little older.

With such recourse the fourth volume started. It cost each subscriber two dollars a year. I suppose the whole volume contained about as much "reading matter," as a cold world calls it, as one number of "Harper's Magazine." These young fellows' reputations were not then made. But as times have gone by, the people who "do the magazines" in newspaper offices would have felt a certain wave of languid interest if a single number of "Harper" should bring them a story and a poem and a criticism by Lowell; something like this from William Story; a political paper by Rufus King; with General Loring, Dr. Washburn, Dr. Coolidge, and Dr. Ellis to make up the number.

Lowell's intimate relations with George Bailey Loring began, I think, even earlier than their meeting in college. They continued long after his college life, and I may refer to them better in another chapter.

The year worked along. They had the dignity of seniors now, and the wider range of seniors. This means that they no longer had to construe Latin and Greek, and that the college studies were of rather a broader scope than before. It meant with these young fellows that they took more liberty in long excursions from Cambridge, which would sacrifice two or three recitations for a sea-beach in the afternoon, or perhaps for an evening party twenty miles away.

Young editors always think that they have a great

NATHAN HALE

deal of unpublished writing in their desks or port-
folios, which is of the very best type, and which,
" with a little dressing over," will bring great credit
to the magazine.   Alas! the first and second numbers always exhaust these reserves.   Yet in the case
of " Harvardiana" no eager body of contributors
appeared, and the table of contents shows that the
five editors contributed much more than half the
volume.

Lowell's connection with this volume ought to
rescue it from oblivion.   It has a curiously old-
fashioned engraving on the meagre title-page.   It
represents University Hall as it then was—before
the convenient shelter of the corridor in front was
removed.   " Blackwood," and perhaps other magazines, had given popularity to the plan, which all
young editors like, of an imagined conference between readers and editors, in which the editors tell
what is passing in the month.   Christopher North
had given an appetite among youngsters for this
sort of thing, and the new editors fancied that
" Skillygoliana," such an imagined dialogue, would
be very bright, funny, and attractive.   But the fun
has long since evaporated; the brightness has long
since tarnished.   I think they themselves found
that the papers became a bore to them, and did not
attract the readers.

The choice of the title " Skillygoliana" was, without doubt, Lowell's own.   " Skillygolee" is defined
in the Century Dictionary in words which give the
point to his use of it: " A poor, thin, watery kind
of broth or soup . . . served out to prisoners in

the hulks, paupers in workhouses, and the like; a drink made of oatmeal, sugar, and water, formerly served out to sailors in the British navy."

Here is a scrap which must serve as a bit of mosaic carried off from this half-built temple : —

SKILLYGOLIANA — III.

Since Friday morning, on each busy tongue,
"Shameful !" "Outrageous !" has incessant rung.
But what's the matter ?   Why should words like these
Of dreadful omen hang on every breeze ?
Has our Bank failed, and shown, to cash her notes,
Not cents enough to buy three Irish votes ?
Or, worse than that, and worst of human ills,
Will not the lordly Suffolk take her bills ?
Sooner expect, than see her credit die,
Proud Bunker's pile to creep an inch more high.
Has want of patronage, or payments lean,
Put out the rushlight of our Magazine ?
No, though Penumbra swears " the thing is flat,"
Thank Heaven, taste has not sunk so low as that !
. . . Has Texas, freed by Samuel the great,
Entered the Union as another State ?
No, still she trades in slaves as free as air,
And Sam still fills the presidential chair,
Rules o'er the realm, the freeman's proudest hope,
In dread of naught but bailiffs and a rope.
. . . What *is* the matter, then ?   Why, Thursday night
Some chap or other strove to vent his spite
By blowing up the chapel with a shell,
But unsuccessfully — he might as well
With popgun threat the noble bird of Jove,
Or warm his fingers at a patent stove,
As try to shake old Harvard's deep foundations
With such poor, despicable machinations. . . .
Long may she live, and Harvard's morning star
Light learning's wearied pilgrims from afar !
Long may the chapel echo to the sound
Of sermon lengthy or of part profound,
And long may Dana's gowns survive to grace
Each future runner in the learned race !

I believe Lowell afterwards printed among his collected poems one or two which first appeared in "Harvardiana." Here is a specimen which I believe has never been reprinted until now : —

> " Perchance improvement, in some future time,
>   May soften down the rugged path of rhyme,
>   Build a nice railroad to the sacred mount,
>   And run a steamboat to the muses' fount !
>
> .   .   .   .
>
>   Fain would I more — but could my muse aspire
>   To praise in fitting strains our College choir ?
>   Ah, happy band ! securely hid from sight,
>   Ye pour your melting strains with all your might ;
>   And as the prince, on Prosper's magic isle,
>   Stood spellbound, listening with a raptured smile
>   To Ariel's witching notes, as through the trees
>   They stole like angel voices on the breeze,
>   So when some strange divine the hymn gives out,
>   Pleased with the strains he casts his eyes about,
>   All round the chapel gives an earnest stare,
>   And wonders where the deuce the singers are,
>   Nor dreams that o'er his own bewildered pate
>   There hangs suspended such a tuneful weight ! "
>
> *From " A Hasty Pudding Poem."*

In the winter of the senior year the class made its selection of its permanent committees and of the orator, poet, and other officers for " Class Day," already the greatest, or one of the greatest, of the Cambridge festivals. I do not remember that there was any controversy as to the selection of either orator or poet. It seemed quite of course that James Ivers Trecothick Coolidge, now the Rev. Dr. Coolidge, should be the orator ; and no opposition was possible to the choice of Lowell as poet.

Some thirty years later, in Lowell's absence from Cambridge, I had to take his place as president of

a Phi Beta Kappa dinner at Cambridge. One of
those young friends to whom I always give the privilege of advising me begged me with some feeling,
before the dinner, not to be satisfied with " trotting
out the old war-horses," but to be sure to call out
enough of the younger men to speak or to read
verses. I said, in reply, that the old war-horses
were not a bad set after all, that I had Longfellow
and Holmes and Joe Choate and James Carter and
President Eliot and Professor Thayer and Dr.
Everett on my string, of whom I was sure. But I
added, " The year Lowell graduated we were as sure
as we are now that in him was firstrate poetical
genius and that here was to be one of the leaders
of the literature of the time." And I said, " You
know this year's senior class better than I do, and
if you will name to me the man who is going to
fill that bill twenty years hence, you may be sure
that I will call upon him to-morrow."

I like to recall this conversation here, because it
describes precisely the confidence which we who
then knew Lowell had in his future. I think that
the government of the college, that " Faculty " of
which undergraduates always talk so absurdly, was
to be counted among those who knew him. I think
they thought of his power as highly as we did. I
think they did all that they could in decency to
bring Lowell through his undergraduate course
without public disapprobation. President Quincy
would send for him to give him what we called
" privates," by which we meant private admonitions.
But Lowell somehow hardened himself to these, the

more so because he found them in themselves easy
to bear.

The Faculty had in it such men as Quincy,
Sparks and Felton, who were Quincy's successors;
Peirce and Longfellow and Channing, all of them
men of genius and foresight; and I think they
meant to pull Lowell through.   In Lowell's case it
was simply indifference to college regulations which
they were compelled to notice.   He would not go to
morning prayers.   We used to think he meant to
go.   The fellows said he would screw himself up
to go on Monday morning, as if his presence there
might propitiate the Faculty, who met always on
Monday night.   How could they be hard on him,
if he had been at chapel that very morning!   But,
of course, if they meant to have any discipline, if
there were to be any rule for attendance at chapel,
the absence of a senior six days in seven must be
noticed.

And so, to the horror of all of us, of his nearest
friends most of all, Lowell was "rusticated," as the
old phrase was.   That meant that he was told that
he must reside in Concord until Commencement,
which would come in the last week in August.   It
meant no class poet, no good-by suppers, no vacation
rambles in the six weeks preceding Commencement.
It meant regular study in the house of the Rev.
Barzillai Frost, of Concord, until Commencement
Day!   And it meant that he was not even to come
to Cambridge in the interval.

I have gone into this detail because I have once
or twice stumbled upon perfectly absurd stories

about Lowell's suspension.   And it is as well to put
your thumb upon them at once.   Thus, I have
heard it said that there was some mysterious offense
which he had committed.   And, again, I have heard
it said that he had become grossly intemperate; all
of which is the sheerest nonsense.   I think I saw
him every day of his life for the first six months of
his senior year, frequently half a dozen times a day,
excepting in the winter vacation.   He lived out of
college; our room was in college, and it was a convenient loafing place.   Now, let me say that from
his birth to his death I never saw him in the least
under any influence of liquor which could be
detected in any way.   I never, till within five years,
heard any suggestion of the gossip which I have referred to above.   There is in the letters boyish
joking about cocktails and glasses of beer.   But
here there is nothing more than might ordinarily
come into the foolery of anybody in college familiarly addressing a classmate.

It is as well to say here that a careful examination of the private records of the Faculty of the
time entirely confirms the statement I have made
above.

CHAPTER IV

CONCORD

CONCORD was then and is now one of the most charming places in the world. But to poor Lowell it was exile. He must leave all the gayeties of the life of a college senior, just ready to graduate, and he must give up what he valued more — the freedom of that life as he had chosen to conduct it. He was but just nineteen years old. And even to the gravest critic or biographer, though writing after half a century, there seems something droll in the idea of directing such a boy as that, with his head full of Tennyson and Wordsworth, provoked that he had to leave Beaumont and Fletcher and Massinger behind him — to set him to reciting every day ten pages of "Locke on the Human Understanding" in the quiet study of the Rev. Barzillai Frost. So is it, — as one has to say that Lowell hated Concord when he went there, and when he came away he was quite satisfied that he had had a very agreeable visit among very agreeable people.

Concord is now a place of curious interest to travelers, and the stream of intelligent visitors from all parts of the English-speaking world passes through it daily. It has been the home, first of all, of Emerson and then of the poet Channing, of Alcott, of

Thoreau, of Hawthorne, known by their writings to almost every one who dabbles in literature. It has been the home of the Hoars, father and sons, honored and valued in government and in law. Two railways carry the stream of pilgrims there daily, and at each station you find two or three carriages ready to take you to the different shrines, with friendly, well-read "drivers" quite as intelligent as you are yourself, and well informed as to the interests which bring you there.

But this page belongs to the last half-century. Lowell went to a quiet country village, the home of charming people, and a type of the best social order in the world; but to him it was simply the place of his exile. Dear Charles Brooks of Newport, who loved every grain of its sand and every drop of its spray, used to say that St. John hated Patmos only because it was his prison. He used to say that John wrote of heaven, "There shall be no more sea," only that he might say, There shall be no chains there; all men shall be free. Lowell looked on Concord as St. John looked on the loveliness of Patmos. His boyish letters of the time steadily called it his prison or the place of his exile.

He was consigned, as has been said, to the oversight and tuition of the Rev. Barzillai Frost, in whose house he was to make his home. Mr. Frost was a scholar unusually well read, who had been an instructor in history in Harvard College, where he graduated in the year 1830. In our own time people are apt to say that Parson Wilbur, of the "Biglow Papers," represents Mr. Frost. I do not recollect that

this was said when they were published. But I dare
say that the little details of Parson Wilbur's life, the
constant reference to the College Triennial Catalogue
and other such machinery, may have come from the
simple arrangements of the Concord parsonage. Mr.
Frost had no sense of congruity. He would connect
in the same sentence some very lofty thoughts with
some as absurd. He would say in a Thanksgiving
sermon, "We have been free from the pestilence
that walketh in darkness, and the destruction that
wasteth at noonday; it is true that we have had some
chicken-pox and some measles."

Imagine the boy Lowell, with his fine sense of
humor, listening to Mr. Frost's sermon describing
Niagara after he had made the unusual journey
thither. He could rise at times into lofty eloquence,
but his sense of truth was such that he would not go
a hair's breadth beyond what he was sure of, for any
effect of rhetoric. So in this sermon, which is still
remembered, he described the cataract with real feeling and great eloquence. You had the mighty flood
discharging the waters of the vast lake in a torrent
so broad and grand — and then, forgetting the precise statistics, he ended the majestic sentence with
the words "and several feet deep."

Lowell could not help entering into conflict with
his tutor, but they were both gentlemen, and the
conflicts were never quarrels. In one of the earliest
letters he says: "I get along very well with Barzillai (your orthography is correct), or, rather, he gets
along very well with me. He has just gone off to
Boston to exchange, and left me in charge of the

'family.' The man's cardinal fault is that he delights to hear the sound of his own voice. When I recite Locke, he generally spends three quarters of the time in endeavoring to row up that delectable writer." To *row up*, in the slang of that time, meant to row an adversary up the Salt River. The phrase was Western. "Sometimes I think that silence is the best plan. So I hold my tongue till he brings up such a flimsy argument that I can stand it, or sit it, no longer. So out I burst, with greater fury for having been pent up so long, like a simmering volcano. However, both he and his wife try to make me as comfortable and as much at home as they can. . . . I think it was Herder who called Hoffman's life a prolonged shriek of thirty volumes. Carlyle borrowed the idea, and calls Rousseau's life a soliloquy of — so long. Now I should call Barzillai's life one stretched syllogism. He is one of those men who walk through this world with a cursed ragged undersuit of natural capacity entirely concealed in a handsome borrowed surtout of other men's ideas, buttoned up to the chin."

This bitterness came in early in the exile. In after times Lowell could speak of Mr. Frost more fairly. In speaking at Concord, on the celebration of the 250th anniversary of the incorporation of the town, he said : —

"In rising to-day I could not help being reminded of one of my adventures with my excellent tutor when I was here in Concord. I was obliged to read with him 'Locke on the Human Understanding.' My tutor was a great admirer of Locke, and thought that he was the greatest Englishman that ever lived, and nothing pleased him more, consequently, than now and then to cross swords with Locke in argument. I was not slow, you may imagine, to encourage him in this laudable enterprise. Whenever a question arose between my tutor and Locke, I always took Locke's side. I remember on one occasion, although I cannot now recall the exact passage in Locke, — it was something about continuity of ideas, — my excellent tutor told me that in that case Locke was quite mistaken in his views. My tutor said: 'For instance, Locke says that the mind is never without an idea; now I am conscious frequently that my mind is without any idea at all.' And I must confess that that anecdote came vividly to my mind when I got up on what Judge Hoar has justly characterized as the most important part of an orator's person."

Of Mrs. Frost, then a young mother with a baby two months old, he says: "Mrs. Frost is simply the best woman I ever set my eyes on. Always pleasant, always striving to make me happy and comfortable, and always with a sweet smile, a very sweet smile! She *is* a jewel! Then, too, I love her all the better for that she loves that husband of hers, and she does love him and cherish him. If she were not married and old enough to be my mother — no! my eldest sister — I'd marry her myself as a reward for so much virtue. That woman has really reconciled me to Concord. Nay! made me even almost like it, could such things be."

By this time, the 15th of August, the poor boy,

though robbed of his vacation, was coming round to see that there were few places in the world where one would more gladly spend the summer than the Concord of his time.

But we must not look in the boy's letters for any full appreciation of Mr. Emerson. While he was at Concord Mr. Emerson delivered an address before the Cambridge divinity school which challenged the fury of conservative divines and was only shyly defended even by people who soon found out that Emerson is the prophet of our century. In one of Lowell's letters of that summer written before that address was printed, and before Lowell had heard a word of it, he says: "I think of writing a snub for it, having it all cut and dried, and then inserting the necessary extracts."

I need not say that this was mere banter. But it shows the mood of the day. Privately, and to this reader only, I will venture the statement that if the most orthodox preacher who reads the "Observer" should accidentally "convey" any passage from this forgotten address into next Sunday's sermon in the First Church of Slabville, his hearers will be greatly obliged to him and will never dream that what he says is radical. For time advances in sermons, and has its revenges.

Lowell speaks of Mr. Emerson as very kind to him. He describes a visit to him in which Lowell seems to have introduced some fellow-students. These were among the earliest of that endless train of bores who in forty years never irritated our Plato. But, alas! Lowell's letter preserves no drop of the honey which fell from Plato's lips. It is only a most amusing burlesque of the homage rendered by the four or five visitors. I may say in passing that the characteristics of the five men could hardly have been seized upon more vividly after they had lived forty years than they appear in the hundred words then written by this bright boy.

In the address at Concord, delivered forty-seven years afterward, he said : —

"I am not an adopted son of Concord. I cannot call myself that. But I can say, perhaps, that under the old fashion which still existed when I was young, I was 'bound out' to Concord for a period of time; and I must say that she treated me very kindly. . . . I then for the first time made the acquaintance of Mr. Emerson ; and I still recall, with a kind of pathos, as Dante did that of his old teacher, Brunetto Latini, 'La cara e buona imagine paterna,' 'The dear and good paternal image,' which he showed me here ; and I can also finish the quotation and say, 'And shows me how man makes himself eternal.' I remember he was so kind to me — I, rather a flighty and exceedingly youthful boy — as to take me with him on some of his walks, particularly a walk to the cliffs, which I shall never forget. And perhaps this feeling of gratitude which I have to Concord gives me some sort of claim to appear here to-day."

Under Barzillai's tuition he settled down to his college work. He had the class poem to write. As he was not to be permitted to deliver it, it may be imagined that he did not write it with much enthusiasm.   He put it off, and he put it off.   That was the way, it must be confessed, he sometimes met such exigencies afterward.

July 8 he wrote: "Nor have I said anything about the poem.   I have not written a line since my ostracism, and, in fact, doubt very much whether I can write even the half of one."   It had been proposed that it should be read by some one else on Class Day; but to this Lowell objected, and the faculty of the college objected also.   On the 23d he writes: "As for the poem, you will see the whole of it when it is printed, as it will be as soon as Scates gets back to superintend it.   Do you know, I am more than half a mind to dedicate it to Bowen." Then on the 15th of August: "I have such a head-ache that I will not write any more to-night, though after I go to bed I am in hopes to finish my poem. Thinking does not interfere so much with a head-ache as writing."   Then, on the next line: "August 18.   The 'poem' is in the hands of the printer.   I received a proof-sheet to-day from the 'Harvardiana' press, containing the first eight pages."   But in the same letter afterwards: "How under the sun, or, more appropriately, perhaps, the moon, which is, or appears to be, the muse of so many of the tuneful, I shall finish the poem I don't know.   Stearns came up here last Saturday, a week ago to-day, and stirred me up about the printing of it, whereupon I began Sunday to finish it in earnest, and straightway scratched off about two hundred and fifty lines. But now I have come to a dead stand and am as badly off as ever, without so much hope.   'Nothing

TO THE CLASS OF '38,

BY THEIR OSTRACIZED POET, (SO CALLED,)

J. R. L.

I.

ssmates, farewell! our journey's done,
Our mimic life is ended,
e last long year of study 's run,
Our prayers their last have blended!

CHORUS.

Then fill the cup! fill high! fill high!
Nor spare the rosy wine!
If Death be in the cup, we 'll die!
Such death would be divine!

II.

w forward! onward! let the past
n private claim its tear,
while *one* drop of wine shall last,
Ve 'll have no sadness here!

CHORUS.

Then fill the cup! fill high! fill high!
Although the hour be late,
We 'll hob and nob with Destiny,
And drink the health of Fate!

III.

at though Ill-luck may shake his fist,
We heed not him or his,
've booked our names on Fortune's list,
So d—n his grouty phiz!

CHORUS.

Then fill the cup! fill high! fill high!
Let joy our goblets crown,
We 'll bung Misfortune's scowling eye,
And knock Foreboding down!

IV.

Fling out youth's broad and snowy sail,
Life's sea is bright before us!
Alike to us the breeze or gale,
So hope shine cheerly o'er us!

CHORUS.

Then fill the cup! fill high! fill high!
And drink to future joy,
Let thought of sorrow cloud no eye,
Here 's to our eldest boy!

V.

Hurrah! Hurrah! we 're launched at last,
To tempt the billows' strife!
We 'll nail our pennon to the mast,
And DARE the storms of life!

CHORUS.

Then fill the cup! fill high once more!
There 's joy on time's dark wave;
Welcome the tempest's angry roar!
'T is music to the brave.

LOWELL'S POEM TO HIS COLLEGE CLASS

so difficult, etc., etc., except the end,' you know. And here I am, as it were, at the tail end of nothing, and not a pillow of consolation whereon to lay the aching head of despair."

These words are perhaps a fair enough description of the poem. It has in it a good deal of very crude satire, particularly a bitter invective against abolitionists who talked and did nothing. But the ode of the Cherokee warrior, bewailing the savage transfer of his nation which had been consummated under Andrew Jackson's rule, seems to be worth preserving. At the time, be it remembered, the poem was most cordially received by the Lilliput circle of Boston and Cambridge: —

> " Oh abolitionists, both men and maids,
>   Who leave your desks, your parlors, and your trades,
>   To wander restless through the land and shout —
>   But few of you could tell us what about !
>   Can ye not hear where on the Southern breeze
>   Swells the last wailing of the Cherokees ?
>   Hark ! the sad Indian sighs a last adieu
>   To scenes which memory gilds with brighter hue,
>   The giant trees whose hoary branches keep
>   Their quiet vigil where his fathers sleep,
>   'Neath the green sod upon whose peaceful breast
>   He too had hoped to lay him down to rest —
>   The woods through whose dark shades, unknown to fear,
>   He roamed as freely as the bounding deer,
>   The streams so well his boyish footsteps knew,
>   Pleased with the tossings of the mock canoe,
>   And the vast mountains, round whose foreheads proud
>   Curled the dark grandeur of the roaming cloud,
>   From whose unfathomed breast he oft has heard
>   In thunder-tones the good Great Spirit's word.
>   Lo, where he stands upon yon towering peak
>   That echoes with the startled eagle's shriek,
>   His scalp-tuft floating wildly to the gale
>   Which howls an answer to his mournful wail,

Leaning his arm upon an unbent bow,
He thus begins in accents sad and low :

"'We must go ! for already more near and more near
The tramp of the paleface falls thick on the ear —
Like the roar of the blast when the storm-spirit comes
In the clang of the trumps and the death-rolling drums.
Farewell to the spot where the pine-trees are sighing
O'er the flowery turf where our fathers are lying !
Farewell to the forests our young hunters love,
We shall soon chase the deer with our fathers above !

"'We must go ! and no more shall our council-fires glance
On the senate of chiefs or the warriors' dance,
No more in its light shall youth's eagle eye gleam,
Or the glazed eye of age become young in its beam.
Wail ! wail ! for our nation ; its glory is o'er,
These hills with our war-songs shall echo no more,
And the eyes of our bravest no more shall look bright
As they hear of the deeds of their fathers in fight !

"'In the home of our sires we have lingered our last,
Our death-song is swelling the moan of the blast,
Yet to each hallowed spot clings fond memory still,
Like the mist that makes lovely yon far distant hill.
The eyes of our maidens are heavy with weeping,
The fire 'neath the brow of our young men is sleeping,
And the half-broken hearts of the aged are swelling,
As the smoke curls its last round their desolate dwelling !

"'We must go ! but the wailings ye wring from us here
Shall crowd your foul prayers from the Great Spirit's ear,
And when *ye* pray for mercy, remember that Heaven
Will forgive (so ye taught us) as *ye* have forgiven !
Ay, slay ! and our souls on the pinions of prayer
Shall mount freely to Heaven and seek justice there,
For the flame of our wigwams points sadly on high
To the sole path of mercy ye 've left us — to die !

"'God's glad sun shone as warm on our once peaceful homes
As when gilding the pomp of your proud swelling domes,
And His wind sang a pleasanter song to the trees
Than when rustling the silk in your temples of ease ;

HARVARD UNIVERSITY.

VALEDICTORY EXERCISES OF THE SENIOR CLASS OF

1838,

TUESDAY JULY 17, 1838.

1. VOLUNTARY. By the Band.

2. PRAYER. By the Rev. Dr. Ware Jr.

3. ORATION. By James I. T. Coolidge. *Boston.*

4. POEM. By James R. Lowell.* *Boston.*

5. ODE. By John F. W. Ware. *Cambridge.*

Tune. *"Auld Lang Syne."*

We meet to part, — no more to meet
Within these sacred walls, —
No longer Wisdom to her shrine
Her wayward children calls.

We met as strangers at the fount
Whence Learning's waters flow, —
And now we part, the prayers of friends
Attend the path we go.

CHORUS.

And on the clouds that shade our way,
If Friendship's star shine clear,
No grief shall dim a brother's eye,
No sorrow tempt a tear.

Yet often when the soul is sad,
And worldly ills combine,
Our hearts shall hither turn, and breathe
One sigh for " Auld Lang Syne."

Then, brothers, blessed be your lot,
May Peace forever dwell
Around the hearths of those we've known
And loved so long, — farewell.

CHORUS.

Farewell, — our latest voice sends up
A heartfelt wish of love, —
That we may meet again, and form
One brotherhood above.

6. BENEDICTION.

* On account of the absence of the Poet the Poem will be omitted.

For He judges not souls by their flesh-garment's hue,
And His heart is as open for us as for you ;
Though He fashioned the Redman of duskier skin,
Yet the Paleface's breast is far darker within !

" ' We are gone ! the proud Redman hath melted like snow
From the soil that is tracked by the foot of his foe ;
Like a summer cloud spreading its sails to the wind,
We shall vanish and leave not a shadow behind.
The blue old Pacific roars loud for his prey,
As he taunts the tall cliffs with his glittering spray,
And the sun of our glory sinks fast to his rest,
All darkly and dim in the clouds of the west ! '

" The cadence ends, and where the Indian stood
The rock looks calmly down on lake and wood,
Meet emblem of that lone and haughty race
Whose strength hath passed in sorrow from its place."

The exile ended with the last week in August.
" I shall be coming down next week, Thursday or
Friday at farthest."

Commencement fell that year on the 29th of
August, and Lowell received his degree of Bachelor
of Arts with the rest of his class.

I believe it is fair to tell an anecdote here of that
summer, because the one person who could be offended by it is himself the only authority for it,
and he used to tell the story with great personal
gusto.

This cynic was in Rome that spring, where Dr.
Lowell and Mrs. Lowell had been spending the
winter. Indeed, I suppose if Dr. Lowell had been
in Cambridge, the episode of rustication in Concord
would never have come into his son's life. The
cynic was one of those men who seem to like to say
disagreeable things whenever they can, and he thus

described, I think in print, a visit he made to Dr. Lowell : —

"Dr. Lowell had not received his letters from Boston, and I had mine; so I thought I would go and tell him the Boston news. I told him that the parts for Commencement were assigned, and that Rufus Ellis was the first scholar and was to have the oration. But I told him that his son, James Lowell, had been rusticated and would not return to Cambridge until Commencement week! And I told him that the class had chosen James their class poet. 'Oh dear!' said Dr. Lowell, 'James promised me that he would quit writing poetry and would go to work.'"

I am afraid that most fathers, even at the end of this century, would be glad to receive such a promise from a son. In this case, James Lowell certainly went to work, but, fortunately for the rest of us, he did not "quit writing poetry."

CHAPTER V

I DESPAIR of making any person appreciate the ferment in which any young person moved who came into the daily life of Boston in the days when Lowell left college. I have tried more than once, and without the slightest success. But this reader must believe me that nobody was "indifferent" then, even if he do not understand why.

Here was a little community, even quaint in some of its customs, sure of itself, and confident in its future. Generally speaking, the men and women who lived in it were of the old Puritan stock. This means that they lived to the glory of God, with the definite public spirit which belongs to such life. They had, therefore, absolute confidence that God's kingdom was to come, and they saw no reason why it should not come soon. There were still some people, and one or two teachers in the pulpit and in what is technically called the religious press, who believed, or said they believed, that all men are born in sin and are incapable of good. But practically, and in general, the people of Boston believed in the infinite capacity of human nature, and they knew " salvation's free," and " free for you and me."

As a direct result of this belief, and of the cos-

mopolitan habit which comes to people who send
their ships all over the world, the leaders of this little community attempted everything on a generous
scale. If they made a school for the blind, they
made it for all the blind people in Massachusetts.
They expected to succeed. They always had succeeded. Why should they not succeed? If, then,
they opened a " House of Reformation," they really
supposed that they should reform the boys and girls
who were sent to it. Observe that here was a man
who had bought skins in Nootka Sound and sold
them in China, and brought home silks and teas
where he carried away tin pans and jackknives.
There was a man who had fastened his schooner to
an iceberg off Labrador, and had sold the ice he cut
in Calcutta or Havana. Now, that sort of men look
at life in its possibilities with a different habit from
that of the man who reads in the newspaper that
stocks have fallen, who buys them promptly, and
sells them the next week because the newspaper tells
him that they have risen.

With this sense that all things are possible to
him who believes, the little town became the headquarters for New England, and in a measure for the
country, of every sort of enthusiasm, not to say of
every sort of fanaticism. Thus, Boston, as Boston,
hated abolitionism. The stevedores and longshore-
men on the wharves hated a " nigger " as much as
their ancestors in 1770 hated a " lobster." But, all
the same, Garrison came to Boston to publish the
" Liberator." There was not an " ism " but had its
shrine, nor a cause but had its prophet. And, as in

the rest of the world at that time, the madness was at its height which forms a " society " to do the work of an individual. People really supposed that if you could make a hundred men give each the hundredth part of his life to do something, the loose combination would do more work than one stalwart man would do who was ready to give one whole life in devotion to the " cause."

The town was so small that practically everybody knew everybody. " A town," as a bright man used to say, " where you could go anywhere in ten minutes."

Cambridge was within forty-five minutes' walk of this little self-poised metropolis, and was really a part of it, in all " its busy life, its fluctuations, and its vast concerns " — and in its pettiest concerns as well.

Lowell could talk with Wendell Phillips, or applaud him when he spoke. He could go into Garrison's printing-office with a communication. He could discuss metaphysics or ethics with Brownson. He could hear a Latter-Day Church preacher on Sunday. He could listen while Miller, the prophet of the day, explained from Rollin's history and the Book of Daniel that the world would come to an end on the twenty-first of March, 1842. He could lounge into the " Corner Bookstore," where James T. Fields would show him the new Tennyson, or where the Mutual Admiration Society would leave an epigram or two behind. Or he could hear Everett or Holmes or Parsons or Webster or Silliman or Walker read poem or lecture at the " Odeon." He

could discuss with a partner in a dance the moral
significance of the Fifth Symphony of Beethoven in
comparison with the lessons of the Second or the
Seventh. Another partner in the next quadrille
would reconcile for him the conflict of free will and
foreknowledge. In saying such things, I am not
inventing the instances. I could almost tell where
the conversations were held. At Miss Peabody's
foreign bookstore he could take out for a week
Strauss's "Leben Jesu," if he had not the shekels
for its purchase, as probably he had not. Or, under
the same hospitable roof, he could in the evening
hear Hawthorne tell the story of Parson Moody's
veil, or discuss the origin of the Myth of Ceres with
Margaret Fuller.[1] Or, when he danced " the pasto-
rale " at Judge Jackson's, was he renewing the
memories of an Aryan tradition, or did the figure
suggest, more likely, the social arrangements of the
followers of Hermann? Mr. Emerson lectured for
him; Allston's pictures were hung in galleries for
him; Mr. Tudor imported ice for him; Fanny
Elssler danced for him, and Braham sang for him.
The world worked for him — or labored for him.
And he entered into the labors of all sorts and conditions of men.

In one of his letters to his friend Loring, written
in October, 1838, he expresses a doubt whether he
would continue his studies of law. "I have been

[1] Margaret Fuller was nine years older than Lowell. A good deal
of her early life was spent in Cambridge; and his banter in the *Fable
for Critics*, which was really too sharp, belongs, not to his man-
hood's serious views, but to a boy's humor.

thinking seriously of the ministry," he writes; "I have also thought of medicine — but there — still worse!" But on the 9th of November "I went into town to look out for a place" — this means to see some of his friends "in business," and to try mercantile life — "and was induced *en passant* to step into the United States District Court, where there was a case pending, in which Webster was one of the counsel retained. I had not been there an hour before I determined to continue in my profession and study as well as I could." Observe that he is now nineteen years old, going on to twenty.

I will not include Mr. Webster among the company of Mr. Lowell's early friends, though the hour spent in the United States Court seems to have been a very important hour in his life. Who shall say what would have come had he "found a place," and begun on life by rising early, "sweeping out the store," filling and trimming the oil lamps, and then running the errands for some treasurer of a woolen factory or dealer in teas or spices? Such was the precise experience of many of his young companions in college, who "elected," on graduation, to "go into business."

Of the literary circles into which he was naturally introduced I will say something. First, of some of the men who, in practice, wrote the "North American Review" in those days — say for the ten years after he left college. Dr. John Gorham Palfrey was the editor, and Lowell would have called the men themselves the "Mutual Admiration Society." Most of them, I think, have recognized this name in their own correspondence. It was a club of five men, who liked to call themselves "The Five of Clubs." But they very soon earned this name of the Mutual Admiration Society, which I think was invented for them.

Dr. Palfrey was living at Cambridge all through the period of Lowell's college and law-school life. He had been a member of the divinity Faculty until 1839, and he assumed the charge of the "Review" in 1835. He had written for it as early as the fifth volume. A gentleman through and through, of very wide information, hospitable and courteous, he and the ladies of his family made his house in Divinity Avenue one of the few places where students of whatever school of the college liked to visit. I remember that one of my own classmates said, after making a Sunday evening call there, "Palfrey makes you think that you are the best fellow in the world — and, by Jove, he makes you think that he is the next best!" He resigned his professorship about the time when he made the romantic voyage by which he emancipated more than forty slaves whom he had "inherited." Like most men with whom he lived, he had opposed the "abolitionists" with all his might, with pen and with voice. But he knew how to do the duty next his hand better than some men who had talked more about theirs.

He was most kind to me, boy and man, and gave me instance on instance which showed that his unflinching firmness in duty was accompanied with entire readiness to recognize the truth wherever he found it. All of us youngsters were enthusiastic about Carlyle. All of the "oldsters" turned up their noses — "such affectation of style," "Germanisms picked up cheaply," and so on. But he said he knew that the editor of the "North American" must read the "French Revolution," and he said that if you had to read a book, a good way was to take it as your only reading when you had a long journey. Mark that you could not then write books on the way, as I am writing this.

So he took his two volumes with him on this voyage of emancipation. And, before he came to Cincinnati, he had forgotten the eccentricities and was as eager as the youngest of us to praise the historian. I remember as well how, as he explained to my father his plans for the "North American Review," he said he had secured Emerson to write, and that Emerson would let him have some of his lectures. He had taken care to provide, however, that these were to be from the historical lectures and not the speculative ones. If he had been pressed, I am afraid he would have been found to be of the large circle of those who in those days thought Emerson "a little crazy."

Under this chief worked the Mutual Admiration Society — all older than Lowell. But with all of them, sooner or later, he became intimate. All of them are still remembered: Charles Sumner; George Stillman Hillard, Sumner's law partner and, in earlier days, intimate friend; H. W. Longfellow; Cornelius Conway Felton, Greek professor at Cambridge, and afterwards president of the college; and Henry Russell Cleveland. Longfellow knew that there were worlds outside of London and Edinburgh, Boston and Cambridge, and their environs. We youngsters, from the proud advantage of the age of twenty or less, would have said that the rest of the Mutual Admiration Society, in the year 1840, did not suspect this.

The "North American" had been founded after the "Monthly Anthology" had led the way, twelve years before. It was confessedly in imitation of the Edinburgh and London quarterlies, as the London Quarterly had confessedly imitated the Edinburgh. The original plan was a good one, and any youngsters of to-day who will revive the old quarterly may find that it meets a "felt want" again. Look at an old "Edinburgh" of Brougham's time and you will find an intelligent account of some forty books, which you will never read yourself, but which you want to know about. To tell the whole abject and bottom truth, you do not find exactly this thing in any English or American "Review" published in 1898.

The "North American" had been under the charge of both Everetts — Edward and Alexander. Alexander Everett assumed the editorial direction on his return from Europe in 1830, and from him it passed into Dr. Palfrey's hands. I may say in passing that if I had at my bank the money which the Everetts and their family connections paid for establishing this national journal, with compound interest on the same, I could be living to-day in my palace at Newport, and entertaining the Duke of Edinburgh, the Bishop of London, and the Vicar-

General of North America. Probably I am better off as I write in the somewhat dingy Albany station of the Delaware and Hudson Railroad. This is a parenthesis, with the indulgence of my readers.

We all read the " North American" regularly. As I have implied, we who were ten years younger than the Mutual Admiration Society made fun of it. We said that they could not review a book of poems without a prefatory essay on poetry. We said that Horace Walpole made their fortune; that they would not publish a number without an article on Walpole. But I cannot now find more than three or four articles on Walpole or even his times in those years.

The truth was that literature was not yet a profession. The men who wrote for the " North American" were earning their bread and butter, their sheets, blankets, fuel, broadcloth, shingles, and slates, in other enterprises. Emerson was an exception; and perhaps the impression as to his being crazy was helped by the observation that these "things which perish in the using" came to him in the uncanny and unusual channel of literary workmanship. Even Emerson printed in the " North American Review " lectures which had been delivered elsewhere. He told me in 1849, after he had returned from England, that he had then never received a dollar from the sale of any of his own published works. He said he owned a great many copies of his own books, but that these were all the returns which he had received from his publishers. And Mr. Phillips told me that when, after "English

Traits," published by him, had in the first six months' sales paid for its plates and earned a balance besides in Emerson's favor, Emerson could not believe this. He came to the office to explain to Mr. Phillips that he wanted and meant to hold the property in his own stereotype plates. And Mr. Phillips had difficulty in persuading him that he had already paid for them and did own them. Emerson was then so unused to the methods of business that Mr. Phillips had also to explain to him how to indorse this virgin check, so that he could place it at his own bank account.

Mr. Phillips, then of the firm of Phillips & Sampson, was Emerson's near connection by marriage; Mrs. Phillips, a charming and accomplished lady, being Emerson's cousin on the Haskins side.

To return to the " North American Review." The five young gentlemen whom I have named were all favorites in the best circles of the charming social life of that little Boston. I cannot see that their fondness for each other can have much affected their work for the " North American," for whatever they published appeared long after they had won their name.

They were in the habit of looking in at what began to be called the " Old Corner Bookstore," which is still, as it was then, an excellent shop, where you find all the last books, the foreign magazines, and are sure of intelligent attention. The memory of modern man does not run back to the time when there was not a " bookstore " in this old building, which bears on its rough-cast wall the date of 1713.

The antiquarians would tell us that on the same spot as early as 1634 there was the first "ordinary" in Boston.   And it was just above here, under the sign of Cromwell's Head, that Colonel George Washington and his elegant little troop made their home when that young Virginian visited Governor Shirley in 1756.

The Corner Bookstore in that generation was the shop of Allen & Ticknor, and not long before there had appeared in the shop, as the youngest boy, James T. Fields, from Portsmouth, who was destined to be the friend of so many men of letters, and who has left behind him such charming memorials of his own literary life.   It must be to Fields, I think, that we owe the preservation of the epigram which the Club made upon "In Memoriam."   I will not say that the story did not improve as it grew older, but here it is in the last edition : —

The firm, then Ticknor & Fields, were Tennyson's American publishers.   They had just brought out " In Memoriam."   One of the five gentlemen looked in as he went down town, took up the book, and said, " Tennyson has done for friendship what Petrarch did for love, Mr. Fields," to which Mr. Fields assented ; and his friend — say Mr. Hillard — went his way.   Not displeased with his own remark, when he came to his office — if it were Hillard — he repeated it to Sumner, who in turn repeated it to Cleveland, perhaps, when he looked in.   Going home to lunch, Sumner goes in at the shop, takes up the new book, and says, " Your Tennyson is out, Mr. Fields.   What Petrarch did for love, Tennyson has

done for friendship." Mr. Fields again assents, and
it is half an hour before Mr. Cleveland enters. He
also is led to say that Tennyson has done for friendship what Petrarch has done for love; and before
the sun sets Mr. Fields receives the same suggestion
from Longfellow, and then from Felton, who have
fallen in with their accustomed friends, and look in
to see the new books, on their way out to Cambridge.

This story belongs, of course, to the year 1850.
In 1841, when Lowell begins to be counted as a
Bostonian, the Corner Bookstore was already the
centre of a younger group of men who were earning
for themselves an honorable place in American letters. I believe they were first brought together in
the government of the Mercantile Library Association. This association started in a modest way to
provide books and a reading-room for merchants'
clerks. To a beginning so simple this group of
young fellows, when hardly of age, gave dignity
and importance. Under their lead the association
established a large and valuable lending library,
set on foot what were the most popular lectures in
Boston, and kept up a well-arranged reading-room.
It was virtually a large literary club, which occupied
a building, the whole of which was devoted to books
or to education. With the passage of two generations much of the work which the association thus
took in hand has devolved upon the Public Library
and its branches and upon the Lowell Institute.
The Mercantile Library has been transferred to the
city and is administered as its South End Branch.

The winter courses under the Lowell foundation take the place of the Mercantile courses, so that this association now shows its existence in a comfortable club-house in Tremont Street.

In the ten years between 1840 and 1850 it was an important factor in Boston life. The initiative in its work was given by James T. Fields, Edwin Percy Whipple, Daniel N. Haskell, Warren Sawyer, Thomas J. Allen, George O. Carpenter, Edward Stearns, and George Warren, who had at command the ready service of younger fellows among their companions, loyal to the interests of the club, and keeping up the best interests of society better than they knew. The club engaged Webster, Everett, Choate, Sumner, Channing, Emerson, Holmes, and Winthrop to lecture to them, arranging for "honorariums" such as had never been heard of before.

The group of officers whom I have named was in itself a little coterie of young fellows who were reading and talking with one another on the best lines of English literature. Fields and Whipple soon became known to the public by their own printed work. All the group were well read in the best English books of the time, and I think I am right in saying that the existence of such a group around him strengthened Fields's hands, as he compelled the firm to which he belonged to introduce in America some of the lesser known English authors. In 1845 Thomas Starr King removed to Boston. His rare genius, insight, and marvelous power of expression gave him a welcome everywhere. In this little circle of the Mercantile Library managers he was the intimate friend of all.

Older than either of these groups of men, there was a set of careful scholars in Boston whom I may distinguish as the historians. Dr. Palfrey once said to me that it was a sort of accident, as he thought, which turned the young literary men of Boston so much in the direction of history. The accident was that the two principal public libraries before 1850 were the Library of the Historical Society, and that of the Boston Athenæum, which was much larger. It so happened that in its earlier years the Athenæum collection was much strongest on the side of history. It also happened that in 1818 Mr. Israel Thorndike bought for Harvard College in one purchase the collection of early American authorities which had been made by Ebeling, a German collector in the first quarter of the century. This collection is still unrivaled. There was thus, so Dr. Palfrey said, a sort of temptation to young Bostonians to read and study American history. And it is almost fair to speak of the Boston " school of history " which was thus formed.

I was a boy of eleven, reading to my mother on a summer afternoon, when my father brought into the room a black-haired, olive-complexioned, handsome young man, and said : " Here is Mr. Bancroft, my dear ! The first volume of the History is finished, and he has come in to talk about printing and publishers." This was the beginning of my acquaintance, I believe I may say friendship, with Mr. Bancroft, which lasted until he died in 1891.[1]

[1] In the preface Bancroft says that he has formed the design of writing our history " to the present time." " The work will extend

It is convenient to remember that he was as old as the century. In 1833, the time of which I speak, Prescott was already at work on "Ferdinand and Isabella." Sparks had edited the "Diplomatic Correspondence," and was collecting the materials for his "Washington." Richard Hildreth, who edited the Boston "Atlas," was preparing for his history of the United States. Palfrey in 1839 gave up his professorship at Cambridge that he might devote himself to the history of New England. Lothrop Motley is younger, but he published "Merrymount" as early as 1848. I may add that the patriotic anniversary orations of both the Everetts are historical studies. Edward Everett, in particular, had the historic sense and tact very delicately developed. Mr. Emerson once said of him that "for a man who threw out so many facts he was seldom convicted of a blunder." To which remark I will add that Mr. Emerson also is always accurate in his frequent references to American history.

It seems best to attempt this sketch of the literary surroundings of the life on which the young law student is now to enter. With every person who has been named, and, indeed, with almost everybody who had anything to do with letters in Boston, Lowell was personally acquainted; with many of them he was intimately acquainted.

to four, perhaps five, volumes." In fact, four volumes carried him to 1776. When he died he had published twelve, which brought him to 1789. One volume of this series, which advances the history only one year, followed its predecessor after two years.

CHAPTER VI

THE BROTHERS AND SISTERS

THERE was an inner circle of companionship, in which Lowell enjoyed the entire love of all the others, some record of which is necessary if we would begin to understand even the outside of his life at that time. I find it hard to determine how far I shall put on paper the memories of this circle. I know very well that it is easy to say too little and easy to say too much.

In college life, especially in their senior year, five of the young men in this company had lived at Cambridge in the closest intimacy. These were Lowell, William Wetmore Story, John Gallison King, William Abijah White, and my brother Nathan. There is no need of saying how this intimacy grew up. White and King were cousins. Story and Lowell were both Cambridge boys, and had been at Wells's school together. Lowell and Hale were together in Alpha Delta and in " Harvardiana." So far I need not try to distinguish this company from companies of college seniors such as many of my readers have known.

But there was a distinction, unique so far as I have seen, in the fact that four of these young men had sisters of nearly their own age, all charming

young women, whose tastes, interests, and studies
were precisely the same as their brothers', and
whose complete intimacy and tender, personal, self-
sacrificing love for each other was absolute. I am
asked by a friend whom I consult with regard to
this narrative to say, what I had not said at first
but what is true, that they were of remarkable personal beauty. No girls ever lived with one heart
and one soul in more complete union and harmony
than these five. They were Anna Maria White,
who married Lowell; Mary Story, who married
George Ticknor Curtis; Augusta Gilman King and
Caroline Howard King, and Sarah Everett Hale.
In their personal talk, in their constant letters, they
spoke of themselves as " The Band." But I need
not say that where there was such an intimacy as
theirs, or where there was such an intimacy as their
brothers', the brothers and the sisters were equally
intimate. The home of each was the home of all.
These homes were in Boston, Watertown, Cambridge, and Salem. Lowell was made as intimate
in each of these homes as he was in his own father's
house. Among all these ten there was the simplest
and most absolute personal friendship.

While the girls called this association " The
Band," the boys were more apt to call it " The
Club." Not that it ever had any place of meeting,
any rules, any duties, or any other conditions of any
club that was ever heard of; but that, generally
speaking, where one of them was, there was another. If one had money, all had it. If one had a
book, all had it. If one went to Salem to a dance,

the probability was that all five went; what was
certain was that two or three went.   If, at the
party, one of the young men was bored by a German *savant* or by a partner he could not leave, he
made a secret signal, and one of the others came to
the rescue.   And so of their sisters.

I am able to speak of the ladies of this group
with the more freedom because four of them died
in early life.   Maria White married Lowell.   Mary
Story, afterwards Mary Curtis, died in May, 1848.
Augusta King and my sister died unmarried.

Whenever they met at Salem, they were sure to
meet also Dr. John Francis Tuckerman, and his sister, Jane Frances Tuckerman.   I suppose any full
catalogue of the Band, if one attempted such a
thing, would include these two names.   But Tuckerman was not a classmate of Lowell's; he was
studying medicine while the others were studying
law, and Lowell was not thrown into such personal
intimacy with him as with the others.

I am favored, by the person best competent to
write, with a few reminiscences: —

DEAR E——: You have asked me to write for
you what I can remember of James Lowell's connection with the Band of Brothers and Sisters.   I will
gladly try to do so, though it would be as impossible
to produce on paper the charm of that brilliant
circle as to catch a falling star and imprison it for
future examination !

But perhaps I can make a picture for you of one
of the Band meetings at my father's house, at which

James Lowell was present, which may give some faint idea of that gay group of friends.

It is in April, 1842, and for weeks sounds of preparation have been echoing through the old house. Two beds are placed in each of the spacious bedrooms, the larder is supplied with dainties, a feeling of expectation pervades the air, and a sense of general festivity is diffused through the house, which has put on its holiday dress to greet the coming guests. As they were all friends of James Lowell's at that time, perhaps a slight sketch of some of them may interest your readers.

First, James himself, slight and small, with rosy cheeks and starry eyes and waving hair parted in the middle, very like Page's picture. He was very reserved in manner, much absorbed in his lady-love, and although his wit was always brilliant, it had not then ripened into the delightful humor of after days. He and his friend William Page, the artist, were at this time possessed with a divine fury for Shakespeare's Sonnets. The little book was forever in their hands, and happy were they when they could catch a stray brother or sister to listen to "just this one beauty," which usually was followed by twenty more; and happy, too, was the brother or sister, for although James did not then read well, his voice being thin and without resonance, his youthful, loving enthusiasm cast a spell over his crooning, the charm of which nobody could resist.[1]

N. H., tall and graceful, perhaps the most highly

---

[1] I have that little volume now, enriched with James's marks and annotations, and full of pleasant memories.

gifted of that bright circle, dropping the diamonds of his polished wit in a languid, nonchalant manner, but capable of a rare awakening when the right moment came.

W. W. S., versatile and vivacious, a capital mimic, an adept at bright nonsense and gay repartee.

W. A. W. A good head and kind heart, always ready to cap a good story with a better, which invariably began with, "I knew a man in Watertown," so that the man in Watertown came to be counted a regular member of the Band.

J. G. K., the leader in the revels, lighting up every meeting with his peculiar racy vein of humor, and J. F. T., the beauty of the Band and the sweetest singer of his time.

And now, with the charming group of sisters, they have all arrived at "The King's Arms" (as they liked to call the cheerful old house) for a week's visit, and I will try to bring back one evening of that happy time.

We were all in a peculiarly gay frame of mind, for a little plan, devised by the sisters to surprise and please James, had proved entirely successful. The "Year's Life" was just published, but had not been as warmly received by the public as we, with our *esprit de corps*, thought it deserved ; so it was arranged that when, on this evening, James, as usual, asked for music, one of the number (our prima donna) should sing one of his own songs, "From the closed window gleams no spark,"[1]

[1] *The Serenade.*

JAMES RUSSELL LOWELL

From the crayon by William Page in the possession of Mrs. Charles F. Briggs,
Brooklyn, N. Y.

adapted to a lovely old air. The song was a great
favorite with both James and Maria, for whom it
was written, and as the well-known words rang
through the room, it was delightful to watch
James's face. Surprise, pleasure, tremulous feeling,
and finally a look of delight as he turned to Maria,
flashed over it. He had been a member of the
Band for only a short time (through his engagement to M. W.), and this friendly appreciation was
doubly valued by both of them.

In those days we always had a fourth meal at
about ten o'clock, and after an evening of music
and dancing, and a good time generally, we adjourned to the dining-room, where, seated at the
large round table, the great festivity began, and an
unfailing flow of wit, sentiment, fun, and scintilla-
tion was kept up into the small hours of the night.
Sometimes James Lowell would be called upon for
one of his two songs, "The Battle of the Nile,"
or "Baxter's Boys They Built a Mill." If "The
Battle of the Nile" were chosen, we prepared for
fun. The words were only,

"The battle of the Nile,
I was there all the while," [1]

in endless repetition, sung to a slow, droning tune.
James had no voice and little ear, though he loved
music. He would begin in a lifeless, indifferent
manner, hardly raising his head, while we all sat

[1] The oldest form of this song is —

"The siege of Belle Isle,
I was there all the while."

This carries it back as far as 1761.

quietly round him. Presently W. S. would join
with his deep bass, then a clear soprano or a tenor
would be heard, and so on, one after another dropping in, until in the end the whole circle would be
on their feet, singing at the top of their voices,
James leading them with all the airs and graces of
a finished conductor. Then James would call upon
my father for his favorite song, —

> " In a mouldering cave where
> The wretched retreat,
> Britannia sat wasted with care.
> She wept for her Wolfe " —

and at this point the whole party were expected to
break out into dolorous weeping. Then came
songs and glees, in the choruses of which we all
heartily joined. Or M. W. would repeat " Binnorie, oh Binnorie," or W. S. sing " A Life on the
Ocean Wave," or some of the party sing and act
for us the oratorio of the " Skeptic," with one
awful chorus, " Tremble Whipstick," in which we
were all expected to show violent signs of trembling
fear. It was all nonsense, but delightful nonsense,
the bubbling over of these gay young spirits.

But this is only a sketch of the lighter hours of
the Band. We had our serious times, when everything in heaven or on earth was discussed with the
airy audacity that belongs to youth, when all the
questions of the day — art, politics, poetry, ethics,
religion, philosophy — were bowled down by our
light balls, with easy certainty that we were quite
able to settle the affairs of the world. There was
great variety of character and opinion among us,

so that our discussions did not lack spice and vigor; but for the short time he was with us, when wit met wit in the bright mêlée, there was no keener lance in rest among the "Knights of the Round Table" than James Lowell's.

CHAPTER VII

A MAN OF LETTERS

LOWELL first saw Maria White on the first of December, 1839. At the moment, I suppose, he did not know that it was preordained that they two should be one. Mr. Norton has hunted out an early letter of his which he wrote the day after that meeting: "I went up to Watertown on Saturday with W. A. White, and spent the Sabbath with him. . . . His sister is a very pleasant and pleasing young lady, and knows more poetry than any one I am acquainted with. I mean, she is able to repeat more. She is more familiar, however, with modern poets than with the pure wellsprings of English poesy." The truth is that their union was made in heaven, that it was a perfect marriage, that they belonged together and lived one life. She was exquisitely beautiful; her tastes and habits were perfectly simple; her education, as I look back on what I know of it, seems to me as perfect as any education can be. Among other experiences which did her no harm, she was one of the frightened girls who fled from the Ursuline Convent in Charlestown before it was destroyed by a mob, in 1834. Her mother was one of the most charming women who ever lived. A cluster of sisters, of all ages down to romping little girls,

MARIA LOWELL

From the crayon by S. W. Rowse, in the possession of Miss Georgina Lowell Putnam, Boston

young women of exquisite sensitiveness and character, and with such a training as such a mother would be sure to give, made the great Watertown house the most homelike of homes. In such a home Lowell found his beautiful wife, and they loved each other from the beginning.

I remember, while I am writing these lines, that all the five young men spoken of in the last chapter entered their names, on graduating, on the books of the Law School. They spent more or less of the next eighteen months at Cambridge. Their intimacy, however, did not spring from this. It might be said, indeed, that they all went to the Law School because they were intimate, rather than that they were intimate because they went to the Law School. Of the five, King only was a professional lawyer through his life. His honored father before him, John Glen King, of the Harvard class of 1807, a learned and scholarly man, had been a distinguished leader at the Essex bar. Story gave most of his life to letters and to art, but his earliest publication is a series of Law Reports, and he afterwards published — in 1844 — a book on Contracts. My brother, after he opened his law office, was early turned away from his profession to the management of the "Daily Advertiser;" and White, who died at the age of thirty-six, before any of the rest of them, gave so much of his time to the temperance and anti-slavery reforms, and to political work, that he cannot be spoken of as a practicing lawyer. None of them are now living.

With another classmate Lowell was on the most

intimate terms — Dr. George Bailey Loring, since distinguished as the head of the Department of Agriculture in Washington. Loring studied medicine at the same time when Lowell went to the Law School; but Lowell frequently visited Loring's beautiful home in Andover, and from schooldays forward the similarity of their tastes brought them into almost constant correspondence in matters of literature. Dr. Loring was the son of the minister of Andover, and that gentleman and Lowell's father had been friends. For us now, this has proved singularly fortunate; for Loring carefully preserved all his letters from Lowell, and Mr. Norton has selected from them many for publication, which throw valuable light upon these early days, in which Lowell really revealed everything to this friend. He was always frank to the utmost with his correspondents, and relied upon their discretion. He was never more annoyed than when a correspondent or an interviewer presumed upon this frankness in repeating, or half repeating, anything, where Lowell had relied on the discretion of a gentleman. Dr. Loring sympathized entirely with Lowell's growing determination to devote himself to literary work, and this sympathy naturally encouraged him, as he broke off, sooner than he perhaps expected, from the practice of law.

Lowell once wrote a funny story which he called "My First Client." I guess that at the bottom it was true. I think that when the painter who had painted his sign came in with his bill, Lowell thought for a moment that he had a client. Out of this he spun an amusing "short story."

This little sketch of his has, in itself, given the impression, perhaps, that he cared nothing about the law, and that his LL. B. on the college catalogue and his admission to the Suffolk bar were purely perfunctory. It is true that he never practiced, and that before long he stopped paying office rent, and that his sign was taken down. But it is not true that he threw away the three years when he pretended to be studying for his profession. In those days the Massachusetts custom was that a young lawyer who sought the best studied for a year and a half at Cambridge under Story and Greenleaf, then spent as much time in a lawyer's office, and then entered at the bar after a formal examination. In this way Lowell spent three or four terms at Cambridge, and then he spent as much time in regular attendance in the office of his father's friend and parishioner, the Hon. Charles Greeley Loring, for many years a leader at the Boston bar. It is not difficult to trace the results of Lowell's faithful work in these three years in his after writing. Any person makes a great mistake who infers from the *abandon* of some of his literary fun that he did not know how to work, steadily and faithfully, better than the worst Philistine who was ever born.

But the stars in their courses did not propose that he should be a chief justice, or a celebrated writer on torts, or that he should make brilliant pleas before a jury. They had other benefits in store for the world.

It is pathetic now to see how little welcome there was then for a young poet, or how little temptation

for a literary career. It was thought a marvel that
the first "New England Magazine" and the "North
American Review" should pay a dollar a page to
their writers. In Longfellow's Life, as in Mr. Lowell's early letters, you find notes of the "Knickerbocker," "Godey," and "Graham," at Philadelphia,
and the "Southern Literary," as willing to print
what was good, but there is evidence enough that
the writers wrote for fame in the intervals spared
them from earning their bread and butter. Holmes
speaks as if he should have lost caste in his profession in those early days had he been known as a
literary man. He even implies that Lowell himself
dragged him back to his literary career.

But better times for American letters or for the
independent profession of literary men were at hand.
"Graham's Magazine" and "Godey's Lady's Book"
had achieved what was called a large circulation.
Stimulated by their success, two young publishers in
Boston, named Bradbury and Soden, determined to
try a magazine in New England which should appeal
for its support to the supposed literary class of the
country, as Blackwood did, and, in America, the
"Portfolio," the "Knickerbocker," and the "Literary Messenger." But it was also to print fashion-
plates, and so appeal to the women of the country,
even if they did not care for literature. So it was
to be called "The Boston Miscellany of Literature
and Fashion." There were to be forty-six pages of
literature, with a good steel engraving, in every
number, and two pages of fashion, with a fashion-
plate.

My brother was to be responsible for the literature, and somebody, I think in New York, for the fashion, with which the former had nothing to do. I remember he had to explain this to Mrs. Stowe, whom he had asked to contribute. She had declined because she had been shocked by a décolletée figure on one of these plates. Dear Mrs. Stowe, in her English progress ten years afterwards, had an opportunity to reconcile herself with dresses much more pronounced.

The "Atlantic" to-day calls itself a journal of literature, art, science, and politics. It does not undertake to reconcile fashion with literature. If Messrs. Bradbury and Soden had been questioned, they would have said, what was true, that there was no class of readers who could sustain creditably a purely literary magazine. The rate at which the poor "Knickerbocker" was expiring was evidence of this. But they would have said that there were a great many factory-girls in the country for whom there was no journal of fashion. They would have said that these girls could be relied upon to float the literary magazine, if in each number there was a love-story which they would be glad to read. And I remember that there was great glee in the counting-room when it was announced that a thousand copies of the new magazine had been sold in Lowell.

My brother was very stiff about concessions to the fashionable side. Two pages might be fashion, and as bad fashion as the publishers wanted, but his forty-six pages were to be the best which he

could command. After a few numbers had been
issued, he made a negotiation with Duyckinck, the
editor of the " Arcturus," by which the short-lived
magazine was transferred to him. This gave him
the help of some of the bright New Yorkers. They
sent to him their accumulated manuscripts, and I
then saw the handwriting of Elizabeth Barrett —
Mrs. Browning — for the first time. Soon after this
these young men in Boston made the personal acquaintance of their New York correspondents, and
from that time began Lowell's close friendship with
Mr. Charles F. Briggs.

Of other writers rising to fame, who were secured
for the " Miscellany," was Hawthorne, who, to the
great pleasure of all of us, contributed the article
" A Virtuoso's Collection." Lowell probably met
him for the first time at Elizabeth Peabody's. Hawthorne soon after married her charming sister. As
a *nom de plume* for a great deal of his work, Hawthorne assumed the French translation of his name.
His stories in the "Democratic Review " of this time
were attributed to " Monsieur d'Aubépine." Lowell
says of him in his Concord address : " You would
think me extravagant, I fear, if I said how highly I
rate the genius of Hawthorne in the history of literature. At any rate, Hawthorne taught us one great
and needful lesson ; and that is, that our own past
was an ample storehouse for the brightest works of
imagination or fancy."

It is interesting now to see that Walt Whitman,
who then called himself Walter, had begun as early
as this his literary career.

CHARLES F. BRIGGS

The page of the " Miscellany " was an imitation as precise as possible of the page which Edward Moxon in London had adopted for several of his popular series. All these young men had read and enjoyed the first part of Browning's " Bells and Pomegranates," which had appeared with Moxon's imprint in this form in 1842.

I speak at this length of the " Miscellany," of which we print a facsimile of one page, because in that year Lowell really made his determination to lead a literary life. It was not the life of a poet simply, but a life of letters, to which from this time he looked forward. To the volume of the " Miscellany " published in 1842 he contributed the following : three articles on " Old English Dramatists," the two sketches " My First Client " and " Getting Up," and, in verse, the sonnet to Keats, " The Two," " To Perdita Singing," " Fantasy," " The Shepherd of King Admetus," and two unnamed sonnets.

In the second number of the " Miscellany," under the date of December, 1841, appeared also the " Ode " which he afterwards thought worth reprinting in the collected edition of his works. One cannot but see in it a careful statement of his own hopes and resolves for his future. It was originally printed in stanzas of four lines ; as he recast it subsequently, the breaks between the stanzas disappear. The following characteristic verses show what was central in his thought and feeling at this time : —

" This, this is he for whom the world is waiting
To sing the beatings of its mighty heart.

Too long hath it been patient with the grating
 Of scrannel-pipes, and heard it misnamed Art.

" To him the smiling soul of man shall listen,
 Laying awhile its crown of thorns aside,
And once again in every eye shall glisten
 The glory of a nature satisfied.

" His verse shall have a great commanding motion,
 Heaving and swelling with a melody
Learnt of the sky, the river, and the ocean,
 And all the pure, majestic things that be.

" Awake, then, thou ! we pine for thy great presence
 To make us feel the soul once more sublime.
We are of far too infinite an Essence
 To rest contented with the lies of Time.

" Speak out ! and lo, a hush of deepest wonder
 Shall sink o'er all this many voicèd scene,
As when a sudden burst of rattling thunder
 Shatters the blueness of a sky serene."

In a private note on the 8th of July he says of
this Ode : " I esteem it the best I ever wrote." And
he adds, " I find that my pen follows my soul more
easily the older I grow. I know that I have a mission to accomplish, and if I live I will do the work
my Father giveth me to do."

At the end of the year, when my brother resigned
the management of the " Miscellany," Lowell and
his friend Robert Carter ventured on the " Pioneer,"
which was to be a magazine of " literature and art."
Fashion was thrown out of the window; and for
illustrations, they began with some good pictures
from Flaxman.

Lowell was already engaged to be married to
Miss White. Their lives were wholly bound up in

CONTENTS.

iii

CONTENTS....Vol. 1.

each other. He was writing to her charming letters in poetry and in prose, and she to him in letters as charming. They read together, they dreamed together, they forecast the future together. In such a daily atmosphere it was natural that he should choose that future rightly.

> " Perhaps then first he understood
> Himself how wondrously endued."

He knew what was in him. By this time he knew he could work steadily, and when he wrote in triumph,

> " I am a maker and a poet,
> I feel it and I know it,"

he wrote in that frank confidence in his future which his future wholly justified.

In the fifth volume of the present series of the " New England Magazine " Mr. Mead has given us a charming article on the three numbers of the " Pioneer." These numbers are now among the rarities most prized by American book collectors. And there is hardly a page of the " Pioneer " which one does not read with a certain interest, in view of what has followed. At the end of three numbers the journal died, because it had not subscribers enough to pay for it. It may be observed in this history of our early magazines that all these publishers lived on what we may call placer gold-washings, for nobody here had yet discovered the quartz rock of an advertising patronage. In the " Miscellany " and the " Pioneer " no enterprising advertiser assisted in the payment of the bills. There was not one advertisement in either. The English magazines printed advertisements long before.

In Lowell's Introductory, written, as will be observed, when he was not yet twenty-four years old, he gives what Mr. Mead well calls a characteristic expression of those views of American literature which always controlled him afterward: " Everything that tends to encourage the sentiment of caste should be steadily resisted by all good men. But we do long for a natural literature. One green leaf, though of the veriest weed, is worth all the crape and wire flowers of the daintiest Paris milliners." The whole article is well worth study by the young critics now.

It is rather funny to see, in these days, that Nathaniel Parker Willis, who then considered himself as the leader of the young literature of America, gave this opinion of Lowell in reviewing the first number of the " Pioneer : " —

" J. R. Lowell, a man of original and decided genius, has started a monthly magazine in Boston. The first number lies before us, and it justifies our expectation, — namely, that a man of genius, who is merely a man of genius, is a very unfit editor for a periodical."

This remark of Willis is interesting now, since Lowell has proved himself perhaps the best literary editor whom the history of American journalism has yet discovered. It is just possible, as the reader will see, that Willis did not write this himself.

Lowell's connection with the " Pioneer " occupied him for the closing months of 1842 and the beginning of 1843. This was at a period when his eyes troubled him badly. Writing from New York, he says: "Every morning I go to Dr. Elliott's (who, by the way, is very kind) and wait for my turn to be operated upon. This sometimes consumes a great deal of time, the Doctor being overrun with patients. After being made stone blind for the space of fifteen minutes, I have the rest of the day to myself."

On the 17th of January he writes, "My eyes, having been operated on yesterday *with the knife*, must be used charily;" and again on the 22d he writes that he had had a second operation performed on the 20th.

"Handbills of the 'Pioneer' in red and black, with a spread eagle at the head of them, face me everywhere. I could not but laugh to see a drayman standing with his hands in his pockets diligently spelling it out, being attracted thereto doubtless by the bird of America, which probably led him to think it the Proclamation of the President, a delusion from which he probably did not awake after perusing the document."

And on the 24th he says: "I can scarcely get through with one letter without pain, and everything that I write retards my cure, and so keeps me the longer here. But I love Keats so much that I think I can write something good about him. . . . If you knew how I am placed, you would not write me so. I am forbidden to write under pain of staying here forever or *losing my eyes*." And in the same letter, "I must not write any more."

"Have you got any copy for the third number?

Do not ask any conservatives to write, for it will mar the unity of the magazine. We shall be surer of success if we maintain a uniform course and have a decided tendency either one way or the other. We shall at least gain more influence in that way."

In New York he often met Willis personally, and the more he saw of him the better he liked him. I think this was what happened with most people who met Willis. It certainly was so with me. In personal intimacy the studied affectation of his printed work disappeared. It was studied, as almost any one could guess without seeing him. Willis also was at this time under Dr. Elliott's care for treatment of his eyes. He told Dr. Elliott that Lowell had written the most remarkable poetry that had been written in this country, and that he was destined to be the brightest star that had yet risen in American literature. He told Lowell himself that he was more popular and more talked about than any other poet in the land, and promised him that he would help the "Pioneer" in every way. At this time Willis was as highly regarded by young people, especially by the sort of people who read magazines, as any literary man in America.

Elizabeth Barrett, not yet married, had written for the Boston "Miscellany," and on the 20th of January Lowell acknowledges four poems from her.[1]

[1] Seeing that Miss Barrett herself recognized the fact that these American magazine publishers were among the first people who ever paid her any money, it is sufficiently English that in the same vol-

There were but three numbers of the "Pioneer" published. It has been the fashion to speak of it in a pitying tone, as if it were a mere foolish enterprise of two callow boys. But if between the numbers or between the articles one reads, as I have done, the correspondence between Lowell and his "true friend and brother," Robert Carter, one feels that the "Pioneer" failed of success only from a series of misfortunes. Looking back upon it now, it is easy to say that it needed capital for a beginning. Most things do in our modern world. It is clear enough in this case that the strongest reason for undertaking it was that Lowell lived and was at the beginning of his successful career. Without him there would have been no "Pioneer." Knowing this, when you find that through January and February he was prohibited from writing, that week after week he was submitting to operations on his eyes, and that he was in actual danger of permanent blindness, you cease to ask why the "Pioneer" died at the end of its third number, and you wonder, on the other hand, that it lived at all.

When one remembers the currency which Lowell's volumes of essays have had from the very beginning, he reads with special interest more than amusement the following note from Miss White, who had seen the publisher, which is pathetic. It describes the persuasion necessary to induce any-

ume of her correspondence which contains her acknowledgment there is talk about "American piracy." One would like to know whether Mrs. Browning did not receive in the long run more money from American than from English publishers.

body to attempt the bold venture of issuing the first in that remarkable series : —

"I went to see Mr. Owen this afternoon, to talk to him about publishing James's prose volume. He expressed himself greatly pleased with the articles, but said he wished to *wait* until James's prose was better known to the public before he ventured upon it. Then I told him of the flattering notices of his 'Old Dramatists' that appeared at the time they came out, and of the lavish praise his prose style received. He said that changed the face of affairs wholly ; that if he were as sure of the public as himself he should not hesitate. He said he wished to see you and talk about it with you also."

Let all young writers remember this, that the public knows what it wants, whether publishers are doubtful or no. I may add the remark, which I believe to be wholly true, of one of the most successful publishers of our day, "No one on earth knows, when a book is published, whether it will sell five thousand copies or not. But if five thousand copies are sold, nothing is more certain than that twenty-five thousand can be."

Mr. Lowell and Miss White were married in the end of December, 1844, with the good wishes, I might say, of everybody. Among her other exquisite faculties she had a sense of humor as keen as his, and both of them would run on, in the funniest way, about their plans for economical housekeeping. Sheet-iron air-tight stoves had just come into being. I believe I never see one to this day without recollecting in what an amusing vein of

List of Copies of the "Conversations" to be given away
by "the Don".

1 W. L. Garrison   with author's respects.
2 C. F. Briggs (~~by Harvard~~) by Wiley & Putnam N.Y. with author's love.
3 Mrs Chapman with author's affectionate regards.
4 T. W. Parsons , Copy of poems & Conversations with author's love.
                    (a note to go with them)
5 John S. Dwight (left at Munroe's bookstore Boston) with author's love.
6 W. Page   with author's love.
7 R. C.   "   "   "
8 Revᵈ Dʳ Lowell   Dedication Copy. ask Owen to send it up.
9 Charles R. Lowell Jr with uncle's love (No. 1. Printed Paces)
10 Revᵈ Chandler Robbins with author's sincere regards (Munroe's bookstore)
13 J. R. L.   3 through Antislavery Offices Care J. M. McKim
14 Mr Nichols (printing Office) with author's sincere regards.
15 { R. W. Emerson with author's affectionate respects.
16 { N. Hawthorne with author's love.
        Both these in one package directed to Hawthorne & left at Miss Peabody's
17 Frank Shaw with author's love.
18 C. W. Story Jr with happy New Year.
        I suppose Mr Owen will allow me 20 Copies as he
did of the poems.
        If the "Don" thinks of any more which I have
forgotten let him send them with judicious inscriptions.
19 "To Miss S. C. Lowell with the best newyear's wishes of her
        affectionate nephew the author."
                    (Mr Owen will send these up.)

20 Joseph T. Buckingham Esqʳ with author's regards & thanks.

absurd exaggeration she once showed, in her lively talk, how much they were going to save in the detail of domestic life by the use of that most unromantic bit of household machinery.

" A Year's Life," his maiden volume of poems, had been published in 1841, about the time of their engagement. We used to pretend that weeks in advance of the publication multitudes of young girls who took a tender interest in this most romantic of marriages walked daily from one to another of the half-dozen book-shops in little Boston to inquire if " A Year's Life " were ready, and thus to stimulate the interest and curiosity of booksellers and their clerks. I think that the larger publishers of to-day even would say that the sale was more than is to be expected from any new volume of short poems. This was, of course, only a retail sale in Boston and the neighboring towns. There was as yet no demand for " Lowell's Poems " in New York, Philadelphia, or London.

Seeing the future of the author's poetical reputation, I think that young authors may be interested in reading the letter in which he first proposes modestly to print this book : —

"I think, nay I am sure, that I have written some worthy things, and though I feel well enough pleased with myself, yet it is a great joy to us all to be known and understood by others. I do long for somebody to like what I have written, and me for what I have written, who does not know me. You and I were cured of the mere *cacoethes imprimendi* (Rufus) by our connection with ' Harvardiana : ' I think that so far we should be thankful to it, as it taught us that print was no proof of worthiness, and that we need not look for a movement of the world when our pieces were made known in print.

"Now, if you will find out how much it would cost to print 400 copies (if you think I could sell so many; if not, 300) in decent style (150 pages — less if printed closely), like Jones Very's book, for instance, I could find out if I could get an indorser. I should not charge less than $1 per vol. — should you? I don't care so much for the style of printing as to get it printed in any way.

"Jones Very's style would be good, too, because it might be printed by our old printers, and that would be convenient about the proofs."

In the subsequent collections of his poems he omitted many of those which are in this pioneer volume. And for this reason, among others, the volume is in great demand among collectors. But it is easy to see that he had even then — two years only after the class poem — outgrown the crudities of younger days which we find in turning over "Harvardiana." There is serious purpose now, though it be expressed only in two or three words together. Some of these are the poems of a lover. Yes! but they are also the poems of a serious young man who knows that there is duty next his hand, and who is determined, with God's help and with the help of her he loves best, to carry that duty through.

The spirit of the book reflects thus the same sense of a mission to mankind which appears in the letters which have been preserved from a full correspondence which he maintained with Heath, a young Virginian. Frank Heath, as his friends called him, graduated at Cambridge while Lowell was in the Law School, and a close intimacy had grown up between them. When Heath left college in August, 1840, he returned to Virginia. There is a careful letter from Lowell to him which has a curious interest now, in the light of the history which followed. Lowell begs him to lead the way and to make himself the typical man in the new history of Virginia by emancipating his own slaves and leading in the establishment of a new civilization there. In fact, Heath soon went to Europe, and was lost to his friends here for nearly twenty years in one or another German university. He returned to his own country in time to take a prominent post in the Confederate army, and I think he lost an arm in one of the battles of the rebellion.

The publication of "A Year's Life" showed that Lowell was a poet. This was now beyond discussion. The papers in the "Miscellany" and the "Pioneer" now showed, what people in the little literary circles of America knew, that he wrote prose well and that he had more than an amateur's knowledge of the older English literature. He could work steadily and faithfully.

In the autumn of 1843 and the winter of 1843–44, however, as has been said, he had trouble with his eyes, and he lived for some time in New York for their better treatment. Mrs. Lowell also, always of delicate health, required a more genial climate than Elmwood or Watertown would give her. Her lungs were delicate, and after their marriage, to escape the harsh climate of Boston, they spent the winter of 1844–45 in Philadelphia. It need not be said that in each city they made very near personal friends who felt and treasured the personal attraction of each of them, — an attraction which it is impossible to describe.

In the same winter the Southern party in Congress and the speculators who had bought Texan bonds for next to nothing were engaged in driving through the last Congress of President Tyler's administration the "joint resolutions" by which Texas was annexed to the United States. There were no precedents for such annexation. What would seem the natural course in an agreement between two republics would have been a formal treaty between them. But it was known that no treaty for such a purpose could pass the United States Senate. It was determined, therefore, by the friends of annexation, who had such support as Mr. Tyler and his Cabinet could give, that they would drive these "joint resolutions" through Congress. And this was done. The resolutions passed the Senate by a majority of one only. They passed the day before Mr. Tyler went out of office. Here was the first pitched battle in Congress on a definite national issue between the North and South since that defeat of the North in the Missouri Compromise which had so excited Charles Lowell the year after his son was born. The whole country, North and South, was wild with excitement, as well it might be.

JAMES RUSSELL LOWELL

From a daguerreotype taken at Philadelphia in 1844

Lowell was ready to give himself to the side of freedom with his pen or with his voice. At this time he engaged in the service first of the "Liberty Bell," an anti-slavery annual published in Boston, and afterwards of the "National Anti-Slavery Standard." Mrs. Lowell also wrote for both journals.

The "Standard" was a weekly journal of great originality and ability, published in New York under the auspices of one of the national anti-slavery societies. The editor was Sydney Howard Gay, afterwards so distinguished as a historian, and holding all his life the most important trusts as a journalist in New York. He worked with Bryant in the "Evening Post." He worked with Greeley in the "Tribune." It is not too late to hope that his memoirs will be collected and published. They will throw a flood of light on points not yet fully revealed in the history of the twenty years which led up to the fall of Richmond and the emancipation of America.

Most organs, so called, of a special philanthropy are narrow and bigoted, and so, by the divine law which rules narrowness and bigotry, are preëminently dull. Witness most missionary journals and all temperance journals, so far as this writer has observed. We owed it to Gay, I suppose, that the "Anti-Slavery Standard," while pitiless in its denunciation of slavery, was neither narrow, bigoted, nor dull. Lydia Maria Child's letters from New York, which were published in it once a week, are still remembered among editors. They give an ideal type for writing in that line, in a series of

papers which may well be studied by young journalists, for, though often imitated, they have never
been equaled.   They are the despair of " leading
editors " who try to get such work done for them
and never succeed.

Lowell engaged himself to write regularly for the
" Standard," and did so for some years.   His prose
papers in that journal have never been collected,
but they would be well worth collection.   And the
poems he wrote at this time, sometimes political, but
not always so, generally appeared in the " Standard."   The headquarters of the young people were
now at Elmwood in Cambridge.   Here their oldest
children were born, and here their oldest child died.
It was then that Maria Lowell wrote that charming
poem which has been read with sympathetic tears in
so many homes from which " the Good Shepherd "
has called away one of his lambs.

I have often heard it said that the " Biglow Papers," which followed soon after, introduced Lowell
in England, and I suppose it was so.   You never can
tell what they will like in England, or what they
will not like.   But this is clear, that, having little
or no humor of their own, they are curiously alive
for humor in others.   And the dialect of the " Biglow Papers," which is no burlesque or exaggeration,
but simply perfect New England talk, is in itself
curious enough and suggestive enough to have introduced letters on any theme.

Literary people in England still fancied that they
were opposed to the principle of slavery, as, in truth,
a considerable number of them were.   And between

the outspoken abolitionists of America and those of
England there was then a freemasonry tender and
charming, though sometimes absurd and amusing.
I suppose this first introduced the Biglow letters,
with their rollicking fun, their absolute good sense
and vigorous suggestions, into England. Once introduced, they took care of themselves, and went
wherever there were readers of sense or even intelligence. They began in a spurt of fun about a little
local passage in Massachusetts politics.

> " Fer John P.
> Robinson he
> Sez he wunt vote fer Guvnor B."

The success of the first numbers naturally led
Lowell to carry them further, and they became in
the end an important factor in the anti-slavery politics of New England.

Meanwhile, as our next chapter will show, what
we now look back upon as the " lecture system " was
developing itself in the Northern States. With the
ordinary stupidity of ecclesiasticism, most of the organized churches had succeeded in shutting out
from their services the ultra speakers on whatever
question. They confined their sermons on Sunday
to the decorous wish-wash in which average men
treated in a harmless way subjects to which the people were indifferent. Speaking of the English pulpit at the same period, under conditions not far different, Jowett says : " Really, I never hear a sermon
of which it is possible to conceive that the writer
has a serious belief about things. If you could but

cross-examine him, he would perjure himself every other sentence." The indifference with which wide-awake Americans, particularly of the younger generation, regarded such preaching, resulted in the development of the "lyceum system" of the North. Of this I will speak in some detail in the next chapter. It is enough to say here that the organized churches might thank themselves if they found, introduced into every community on week-days, the most radical views, and frequently by speakers who would not have pretended to address them on Sundays. I am trying not to travel outside the line which I have marked for myself in these papers; but I do not pass that line when I say that a sort of indignation was aroused through the whole Northern community because the established church, in its various communions, was unwilling to devote itself to what was clearly its business, the fair discussion of the most important subject bearing on right and wrong which could possibly come before any people. The reader will find some valuable notes by Mr. Higginson, interesting of course, in "Cheerful Yesterdays." "All of which he saw, and much of which he was."

I refer to this now not because Lowell was often engaged in lecturing as one of the anti-slavery speakers. It must be remembered that this book is not so much a history of his life, as an effort to show the circumstances which surrounded his life and which account for the course of it. In his weekly contributions to the press, whether in prose or in verse, he kept in touch with the men and women who were quite in advance in forming the Northern or national sentiment of the crisis.

The " Liberty Bell " and the " Standard," with his bright and suggestive articles, went into the circles which summoned Parker and Phillips and Garrison to give them instruction or inspiration which they would have sought in vain from the more decorous pulpits of that day. So it happened that, although he did not " enter the lecture field " as early as some of his companions and friends in the anti-slavery cause, he was, in those years of the awakening, perfectly well known among those interested in that cause.

In this connection it interests me to remember that the last time I saw his father, Dr. Lowell, was at the house in Elmwood in 1855. I went to him to ask for his assent and signature in a memorial relating to the freedom of Kansas, which was addressed to what we then called " The Three Thousand New England Clergymen." I went to him because he was one of the oldest Congregational ministers in New England, and because he had always deprecated the separation between the evangelical and liberal branches of that body. He sympathized heartily in what we were doing, signed his name at the head of our circular-letter, and then put his hand on my head, and in the most cordial and pathetic way gave me and our cause an old man's benediction. This, the reader should note, took place in the spring of 1855.

CHAPTER VIII

IT will be as well to bring into one chapter such references to Lowell's work as a public speaker as may give some idea of the interest with which he was always heard, and, indeed, of his own evident enjoyment of the position of an orator.

He spoke with absolute simplicity, with entire ease, and he really enjoyed public speaking.

It was near the close of the first quarter of the century that what was called the " lyceum system " came into being in New England. It worked wonderfully well under the original plans. The institution, as it may be called, or the habit, if you please, of lecturing and listening to lectures, was formed again, probably never to be abandoned in our communities. The method by which this was done in the New England towns worked well for a generation. And Lowell, as a youngster starting on life, made some of his first addresses " under the auspices " of the old-fashioned lyceum committees.

I am rather fond of saying, what nobody seems to care for excepting myself, that high among the causes which sent Winthrop's colony to Massachusetts was the passion of such men as he to hear lectures on week-days. Now this was important.

It means that the contest between the "left wing"
and the "right wing" in the English Church turned
largely on the wish of the more advanced clergy to
speak in other pulpits than their own, and the greater
wish of the Puritan people to hear them. Of course,
if a bishop could shut up a man in his own pulpit,
the influence of one of the Garrisons, or Phillipses,
or Parkers, or Pillsburys of the day would be very
much restricted. But so long as John Cotton could
travel over half England, he was much more for-
midable to Bishop Laud and the other people who
directed the Establishment than he would have
been if he had remained in his own pulpit in the
Lincolnshire Boston.

So there grew up for that generation the habit of
a week-day lecture in the New England meeting-
houses; a habit preserved with more or less interest
to the present day. But as time went by, these
week-day lectures, so far as I recollect them, were
little more than the repetition of sermons which had
been preached on Sunday. Now, if there is anything dangerous anywhere for a lecturer's usefulness,
it is a habit of repeating the average sermon. A sermon is one thing and a lyceum lecture is another. A
lyceum lecture has one purpose, and a sermon ought
to have another purpose. However this may be, the
people of the generations of this century who did
not much like to go to the "Thursday lecture" in
Boston, or similar lectures in other towns, were very
glad to hear the best speakers of the time. And
they generally gave them more latitude than was to
be found in the creed-bound churches of the time.

I do not think I stray too far from our central subject if I take a few lines to speak of the value to the whole Northern community of this very curious system. To introduce such men as have been named above, and a hundred other men, some of them of equal prominence in our history, and all of them of a certain ability as public speakers, — to introduce such men to the average community of the North, so that it knew them personally, was in itself a great achievement. To go back to the comparison which I have made already, these Peter the Hermits, passing from place to place, preached a crusade. They were in very much the position of John Cotton and those other Puritan lecturers whom Bishop Laud and the Star Chamber disliked in England. And the history of the twenty years before our Civil War is not rightly written unless it refers to the effect which was wrought by such speakers. Phillips, Parker, Ward Beecher, and even Garrison, would have been little known outside a small circle around their respective homes but for this lecturing practice.

There will be found in Lowell's letters and in other memoranda of the time an occasional joke about the external hardships of the thing. He speaks somewhere of three " committeemen," with three cold hands like raw beefsteak, welcoming him and bidding him good-by. But such little jokes as this must not give a false idea of the reception which was given to the pioneers of larger thought than that which the hidebound churches of the time were willing to interpret. For one such story

of the beefsteak hands there could be told a thousand stories of warm welcomes into charming families, and of immediate mutual recognition of people
of kindred thought who would never have seen each
other's faces but for the happy appointment which
brought one as a lecturer to the other as " commit-
teeman." Anything that taught the separated people of this country that it was a country, that they
were citizens of the same nation, and that they had
each other's burdens to bear, was of great value in
those days. The reader of to-day forgets that in
the same years in which South Carolina was defy-
ing the North, Massachusetts gave directions that
the national flag should not float over her State
House. That is to say, in those days there was an
intense sensitiveness which kept men of different
sections of the country apart from each other.
Anything which overcame such sensitiveness, and
brought real lovers of their country and lovers of
God face to face, was an advantage. In this case
the advantage can hardly be overestimated.

To this hour the popular lecture in America dif-
fers from the lecture, so called, which the Useful
Knowledge Society of England, and what they used
to call Mechanics' Institutes, established there in
the earlier part of the century. Mr. Emerson told
me that when he delivered his lectures in London,
intelligent people went back to Coleridge's morning
lectures, of a dozen or more years before, as a pre-
cedent. And you see in the accounts of Carlyle's
London lectures that it was regarded as a novelty
that anything should be said at a lecture which

decently intelligent people needed to hear. But in
October, 1843, Emerson wrote to his friend John
Sterling, " There is now a ' lyceum,' so called, in
almost every town in New England, and if I would
accept an invitation I might read a lecture every
night." Sterling had written to him not long before, " I doubt whether there are anywhere in Britain, except in London, a hundred persons to be
found capable of at all appreciating what seems to
find, as spoken by you, such ready acceptance from
various bodies of learners in America." Such people meet, in their moribund feudal fashion, " to
encourage the others," as Sir Walter Vivian looked
on the experiments in his own park, or as Murat
charged at Borodino. The amusing condescension,
so often observable in the English pulpit, is even
more marked in the English " popular lecture."

But, in the beginning, it was not so here. As
early-as 1814 Jacob Bigelow had lectured on botany
in Boston, and, not long after, Edward Everett on
Greek art and antiquities, and Henry Ware on the
Holy Land, in courses of lectures, which were attended by the very best and most intelligent people.
And when Waldo Emerson, and Theodore Parker,
and Wendell Phillips, and James Lowell lectured in
the same region, they gave the best they could give,
and no one thought he condescended in going to
hear.

I do not forget a bright saying of Starr King,
one of those best worth hearing of the brilliant
group of traveling lecturers of whom Lowell was
one. King said that a popular lyceum lecture

was made of five parts of sense and five of nonsense. " There are only five men in America,"
said he, " who know how to mix them — and I
think I am one of the five." Other people thought
so too, and did not detect the nonsense. His carefully wrought lectures are worth anybody's study
to-day.

He is the author of another lyceum chestnut.
Some one asked him what his honorarium was for
each lecture. " F. A. M. E.," said he — " Fifty
And My Expenses."

Lowell's hearers got no nonsense. His subjects
were generally literary or critical — I think always
so. On one or more expeditions he went to what
was then the Far West — speaking in Wisconsin, I
observe, within twenty years after Black Hawk and
Keokuk addressed Americans on the same fields.

(Ah me ! Why did I not accept forty acres of
land between the lakes in Madison, Wisconsin, when
they were offered me in 1842? The reader will
perhaps pardon this digression !)

Of such a system of Wanderjähre in the education of a country, not the least benefit is that which
is gained by the speaker. No man knows America
who has not traveled much in her different regions.
A wise United States Senator proposed lately that
each newly elected member of Congress should be
compelled to travel up and down his own country
for those mysterious months after his election before
he takes his seat. The men who have had such a
privilege do not make the mistakes of book-trained
men.

A good enough illustration of some of the deeper consequences of what may be called the lyceum movement may be found in the story often told of the divided committee who met Wendell Phillips in a place where he was quite a stranger. On his arrival he asked what was the subject he was to speak on. Should he read his lecture on the Lost Arts, or should he deliver an address on Anti-Slavery? It proved, alas! that the committee was equally divided, perhaps bitterly divided, and neither side would yield to the other. Phillips at once made the determination with his own prompt wit. He said he would deliver the lecture on the Lost Arts first, and then the Anti-Slavery address afterwards for any who wanted to stay and hear. Of course, after they had heard him, everybody stayed, and so he had the whole town to hear his radical appeal, where otherwise he would have had only that half the town which was convinced already.

Under a law which may be called divine, the students, in all colleges where they had the choice of anniversary orators, always elected the speakers who, as they thought, would be most disagreeable to the college government. So Emerson, Parker, and Phillips came to be favorite college speakers in colleges where the faculties would gladly have suppressed all knowledge of the men. Mr. Emerson's address at Dartmouth in 1838 would never have been delivered but for the action of this law. This address, when printed, lying on the counter of a book-shop in Oxford, gave to Gladstone his first knowledge of the New England Plato.

It is amusing now, and in a way it is pathetic, to
see how this youngster Lowell, even before he was
of age, caught at the floating straw of a Lyceum
engagement whenever he could, in the hope of earning a little money. This was simply that he felt
the mortification which every bright boy feels when,
after being told that he is a man by some college
authority, he finds that he is still living in his
father's house, eating at his father's table, wearing
clothes which his father pays for, and even asking
his father for spending-money. There is a note
from him to Loring to ask if the "Andover Lyceum" will pay as much as five dollars for a lecture.

The reader must understand that in the "Lyceum
system," so called, it was considered as a sort of
duty for educated men to have on hand a lecture or
two which they were willing to read to any audience
which was willing to ask them. This was, by the
way, in precise fulfillment of that somewhat vague
commission which constitutes the degree of a Master
of Arts. The person who is fortunate enough to
receive this diploma is told that he has the privilege
of "speaking in public as often as any one asks him
to do so." This is my free translation of "publice
profitendi." Those words never really meant
"public profession." In our modern days we are a
little apt to take this privilege without the permis-
sion of the university.

Educated men accepted such appointments as
their contribution to public education. It was just
as the same men served on the school committee or
board of selectmen, and would have been insulted

if anybody had proposed to pay them anything for
doing it.   In many cases, perhaps in most cases, no
tickets were bought or sold.   The selectmen gave
the Town Hall for a lyceum, or the First Parish
gave the use of its meeting-house for a lyceum, as
they would have done for a temperance meeting or
a missionary meeting.   But, of course, it soon appeared that if the audiences were to have continuous
courses of lectures, somebody must be paid for them,
and somebody must pay.   College professors were
engaged to give elementary courses on scientific or
historical subjects.   As early as 1832 Mr. Emerson
delivered a course of biographical lectures at the
request of the Massachusetts Society for Diffusing
Useful Knowledge.   And in the years of the 30's
in Boston there were maintained through the winter
public courses almost every evening in the week, by
at least five different organizations — the Society for
Diffusing Useful Knowledge, the Boston Lyceum,
the Mercantile Library Association, the Mechanics'
Association, and sometimes the Historical Society.
For all these courses tickets were sold at low rates,
but for enough to enable the societies to pay the
lecturers a small honorarium.   From such arrangements as these the custom spread of recompensing
the lecturer for his work; and at this moment, in
an average New England town, people will not go
to a lecture if they think the lecturer has "given"
his service.   The public thinks that if not worth
pay, it is not worth hearing.

In this arrangement of the lyceum, Lowell found
his place before he was of age.   He was always an

easy and a ready speaker, and, as I have said, he enjoyed public speaking. Before long, his interest in the temperance reform and the anti-slavery reform brought him occasionally on the platform. He spoke with perfect ease. On such occasions he spoke without notes, never speaking without knowing what he had to say, and always saying it. But I think he never delivered a lecture, as he would have called it, without a manuscript written out in full.

The first account he gives of his public speaking is that of the celebration of the Cambridgeport Women's Total Abstinence Society on the Fourth of July, 1842. " There were more than three thousand in all, it was said. I was called out, and made a speech of about ten minutes, from the top of a bench, to an audience of two thousand, as silent as could be. I spoke of the beauty of having women present, and of their influence and interest in reforms. I ended with the following sentiment: 'The proper place of woman — at the head of the pilgrims back to purity and truth.' In the midst of my speech I heard many demonstrations of satisfaction and approval — one voice saying, 'Good!' in quite an audible tone. I was told that my remarks were 'just the thing.' When I got up and saw the crowd, it inspired me. I felt as calm as I do now, and could have spoken an hour with ease. I did not hesitate for a word or expression even once."

Alas! the Boston papers of the day had Mr. Tyler's " third veto " to print, and the news from England by a late arrival; and no word could be

spared for poor James's first essay. What saith the
Vulgate? "Nullum prophetam in actis diurnis
honorari."

As it proved, he was brought face to face with
large numbers of persons who would otherwise never
have seen him, by delivering lectures in various
courses through the Northern and Northwestern
States; but this did not begin until a period as late
as 1855. What I have said of his easy speaking is
the remark of a person who heard him, as I have
often heard him. I never spoke with any one who
had heard him who did not say the same thing.
But he himself did not always feel the sort of confidence in his power in this way which would have
seemed natural. I am told by many persons who
had to introduce him upon such occasions, that he
would be doubtful and anxious about his power with
an audience before he began. And he was exces-
sively sensitive about any accident by which he for-
got a word or in any way seemed to himself to have
tripped in his discourse.

In 1853 he was invited to deliver a course of lectures before the Lowell Institute. These lectures
were eventually delivered in January and February
of 1855.

Because the great system of public instruction
which is carried on by this Institute bears the name
of his family, I will give some little account of it
here. Stimulated by the success of what we have
been speaking of, the lyceum system of the Northern States, John Lowell, Jr., a cousin of James
Russell Lowell, had founded this Institute. His

JOHN LOWELL, JR.

From a painting by Chester Harding, in the possession of Augustus Lowell, Boston

wife and all his children had died.   His own health
was delicate, and he undertook a long journey
abroad.   While in Egypt he made his will, in which
he left $250,000 for the beginning of a fund for
carrying on public instruction by means of lectures.
It is said that it was executed literally under the
shadow of the ruins of Luxor.

By this instrument he left to trustees the sum
which has been named, the interest of which should
be expended for maintaining free public lectures for
the instruction of any who should choose to attend.
The will provided that nine tenths of the income
should be thus expended for the immediate purposes
of every year.   The remaining tenth is every year
added to the principal fund.   The investments have
been carefully and successfully made, and as the will
went into effect in the year 1839, the fund is now
very much larger than it was when he died.

It has been admirably administered from the
beginning.   The first Americans in the walks of
science or of literature have been proud to be
enrolled on the list of its lecturers, and in many
instances the most distinguished savants from Europe have been called over with the special purpose
of lecturing to its audiences.

Before 1855 Lowell was, I may say, universally
known and universally admired.   The announcement that he was to deliver a course of twelve
lectures on English poetry was gladly received in
Boston.   It proved at once that it would be necessary to repeat the lectures in the afternoons for a
new audience of those who could not enter the hall

in the evening. But in both afternoon and evening courses multitudes were turned away for whom there was no room in the hall. A much larger "audience" was made up by the people who read the lectures from day to day in the newspaper. My father and brother, who then conducted the "Daily Advertiser," arranged with Mr. Lowell that his old friend Mr. Robert Carter should prepare the manuscript for that paper, and thus the "Advertiser" printed each lecture on the day after its second delivery, with the omission only of some of the extracts from the poets of whom he was speaking.

These reports were carefully preserved by some scrap-book makers, and from one of the scrap-books thus made the Rowfant Club of Cleveland printed an elegant limited edition in 1897.

I borrow from another the description of Mr. Lowell's manner as a speaker in delivering these and similar addresses. This writer, who is not known to me, says, first, that Mr. Lowell never imitates the stump speaker and never falls into the drollery of the comedian. "His pronunciation is clear and precise; the modulations of his voice are unstudied and agreeable, but he seldom if ever raised a hand for gesticulation, and his voice was kept in its natural compass. He read like one who had something of importance to utter, and the just emphasis was felt in the penetrating tone. There were no oratorical climaxes, and no pitfalls set for applause."

The subjects of the twelve lectures are these: 1. Definitions. 2. Piers Ploughman's Vision. 3. The

JOHN HOLMES, ESTES HOWE, ROBERT CARTER, JAMES RUSSELL LOWELL

From a photograph owned by General James Lowell Carter

Metrical Romances. 4. The Ballads. 5. Chaucer. 6. Spenser. 7. Milton. 8. Butler. 9. Pope. 10. Poetic Diction. 11. Wordsworth. 12. The Function of the Poet.

It is no wonder that the lectures were so popular. They are of the best reading to this day, full of fun, full of the most serious thought as well. And you find in them at every page, I may say, seeds which he has planted elsewhere for other blossoms and fruit. For instance, here is his description of a New England spring : —

"In our New England especially, where May-day is a mere superstition and the May-pole a poor, half-hardy exotic which shivers in an east wind almost as sharp as Endicott's axe — where frozen children, in unseasonable muslin, celebrate the floral games with nosegays from the milliners, and winter reels back, like shattered Lear, bringing the dead spring in his arms, her budding breast and wan, dilustered cheeks all overblown with the drifts and frosty streaks of his white beard — where even Chanticleer, whose sap mounts earliest in that dawn of the year, stands dumb beneath the dripping eaves of his harem, with his melancholy tail at half-mast — one has only to take down a volume of Chaucer, and forthwith he can scarce step without crushing a daisy, and the sunshine flickers on small new leaves that throb thick with song of merle and mavis."

We find much of this again in the "Biglow Papers;" perhaps the prose is better than the verse. Indeed, you have only to turn over the pages to find epigrams of which you might make proverbs.

" Fortunately for the ballad-makers, they were not encumbered with any useless information." " The ballads are pathetic because the poet did not try to make them so; and they are models of nervous and simple diction, because the business of the poet was to tell his story and not to adorn it." " The only art of expression is to have something to express. We feel as wide a difference between what is manufactured and what is spontaneous as between the sparkles of an electrical machine and the wildfire of God which writes ' *Mene, Mene,*' on the crumbling palace walls of midnight cloud." " Even Shakespeare, who comes after everybody has done his best, and seems to say, ' Here, let me take hold a minute and show you how to do it,' could not mend that."

Let no one suppose, because these lectures are thus delivered to what is called a popular audience, that there is anything slight in the work or superficial in the handling. Lowell was not the man to slight his work because he had an audience of the people, or to treat the rank and file with more superficial consideration than the men with epaulets or sashes. Even if he had been, when he delivered one of these courses of lectures he had before him his full share of the leaders of that community, men and women to whom even a Philistine would not dare bring the work of a slop-shop.

A good deal of the thought of these lectures appears, as I have said, in other forms in some of his later publications. But, for whatever reason, he never made a separate book of them. I think he says somewhere in a private letter that he wanted to do it, and indeed had meant to do it, but that he could not make the time ; and that this was a fair excuse any one will say who knows how steadily he worked and how much work he had to do in study, in teaching, in writing and proof-reading, and, in after life, in his diplomatic duties.

In 1874 Mr. Lowell was chosen the President of the Harvard Society of Alumni, and from 1863 to 1871 he was President of the Phi Beta Kappa of Cambridge. It is worth observing that no other President of the Phi Beta has ever held that position so long. His immediate predecessor was Judge Hoar, and his successor Richard Henry Dana. These two societies exist chiefly to provide for the annual dinners of Cambridge graduates at the College on Commencement Day and the day following. The fine charm of the Phi Beta dinner is that it is not expected or permitted that anything that is said shall be reported. You may look for the most bubbling fun of some of the most serious men in the world, without any terror of seeing it bewitched and reflected the next morning from the cracked mirror of some ignorant boy who, when he reads his notes, can see no difference between Voltaire and Valkyrie. But the Commencement dinners, the day before the Phi Beta dinners, are open to the reports of all men, angels, and devils, so that some of the sparks of Lowell's infinite fun may, with proper grinding, be thrown upon the kodak still.

He officiated as President of the Alumni in 1875 and 1876. Those years, as the centennial years of

the early Revolutionary events, kept every one on
the alert as to New England history.   Here is a
short extract from each of these addresses : —

"But, gentlemen, I will not detain you with the
inevitable suggestions of the occasion.   These sen-
timentalities are apt to slip from under him who
would embark on them, like a birch canoe under
the clumsy foot of a cockney, and leave him floun-
dering in retributive commonplace.   I had a kind of
hope, indeed, from what I had heard, that I should
be unable to fill this voice-devouring hall.   I had
hoped to sit serenely here, with a tablet in the wall
before me inscribed : ' Guilielmo Roberto Ware,
Henrico Van Brunt, optime de Academia meritis, eo
quod facundiam postprandialem irritam fecerunt.'
[The reader must recognize here the distinguished
architects of Memorial Hall, which was then newly
built.]   I hope you understood my Latin, and
I hope you will forgive me the antiquity of the
pronunciation, but it is simply because I cannot
help it.   Then, on a blackboard behind me, I could
have written in large letters the names of our
guests, who should make some brave dumb show of
acknowledgment.   You, at least, with your united
applause, could make yourselves heard.   If brevity
ever needed an excuse, I might claim one in the
fact that I have consented, at short notice, to be
one of the performers in our domestic centennial
next Saturday, and poetry is not a thing to be delivered on demand without an exhausting wear upon
the nerves.   When I wrote to Dr. Holmes and
begged him for a little poem, I got the following

answer, which I shall take the liberty of reading. I do not see the Doctor himself in the hall, which encourages me to go on : —

" ' My dear James, — Somebody has written a note in your name, requesting me to furnish a few verses for some occasion which he professes to be interested in.   I am satisfied, of course, that it is a forgery.   I know you would not do such a thing as ask a brother writer, utterly exhausted by his centennial efforts, to endanger his health and compromise his reputation by any damnable iteration of spasmodic squeezing.   So I give you fair warning that some dangerous person is using your name, and taking advantage of the great love I bear you, to play upon my feelings.   Do not think for a moment that I hold you in any way responsible for this note, looking so nearly like your own handwriting as for a single instant to deceive me, and suggesting the idea that I would take a passage for Europe in season to avoid college anniversaries.'

" I readily excused him, and I am sure you will be kind enough to be charitable to me, gentlemen. I know that one of the things which the graduates of the College look forward to with the most confident expectation and pleasure is the report of the President of the University.   I remember that when I was in the habit of attending the meetings of the faculty, some fourteen or fifteen years ago, I was very much struck by the fact that almost every field of business that required particular ability was sure to gravitate into the hands of a young professor of chemistry.   The fact made so deep an impression

upon me that I remember that I used to feel, when
our war broke out, that this young professor might
have to take the care of one of our regiments, —
and I know he would have led it to victory. And
when I heard that the same professor was nominated
for President, I had no doubt of the result which
we have all seen to follow. I give you, gentlemen,
the health of President Eliot, of Harvard College!"

Holding the same honorable though honorary
office the next year, before introducing the speakers,
he said: —

"The common consent of civilized mankind seems
to have settled on the centennial commemoration of
great events as leaving an interval spacious enough
to be impressive and having a roundness of comple-
tion in its period. We are the youngest of nations,
and the centuries to us are not yet grown so cheap
and so commonplace as Napoleon's, when he saw
forty of them looking down in undisguised admiration upon his armies bronzed from their triumphs in
Italy. For my own part, I think the scrutiny of
one age is quite enough to bear, without calling in
thirty-nine others to its assistance. It is quite true
that a hundred years are but as a day in the life of
a nation, are but as a tick of the clock to the long
train of æons in which this planet hardened itself for
the habitation of man and man accommodated himself to his habitation; but they are all we have, and
we must make the best of them. Perhaps, after all,
it is no such great misfortune to be young, especially
if we are conscious at that time that youth means
opportunity and not accomplishment. I think that,

after all, when we look back upon the hundred years through which the country has passed, the vista is not so disheartening as to the indigestive fancy it might at first appear. If we have lost something of that Arcadian simplicity which the French travelers of a hundred years ago found here, — perhaps because they looked for it, perhaps because of their impenetrability by the English tongue, — we have lost something also of that self-sufficiency which is the mark as well of provincials as of barbarians, and which is the great hindrance to all true advancement. It is a wholesome symptom, I think, if we are beginning to show some of the talent for grumbling which is the undoubted heirloom of the race to which most of us belong. Even the Fourth of July oration is changing round into a lecture on our national shortcomings, and the proud eagle himself is beginning to have no little misgiving as to the amplitude between the tips of his wings. But while it may be admitted that our government was more decorously administered one hundred years ago, if our national housekeeping to-day is further removed from honest business principles, and therefore is more costly, morally and financially, than that of any other Christian nation, it is not less true that the hundredth year of our existence finds us, in the mass, very greatly advanced in the refinement and culture and comfort that are most operative in making a country civilized and keeping it so."

On three occasions, at least, Lowell substituted for a prose lecture a poem to which he gave the name of "The Power of Sound." It is constructed

on the simple system which runs back as far as
" The Pleasures of Imagination," giving us, for
instance, the " Pleasures of Hope " and the " Pleasures of Memory." In these prehistoric days of
which I write, it was what you rather expected in a
college poem: a convenient thread on which to
string the beads which might else have been lying
unused in box or basket.

Lowell gave the original copy of this poem to
Mr. Norton, who edited it carefully with interesting
notes for an elegant edition of a few copies printed
by Mr. Holden. Some of the lines and several of
the illustrations in other forms were used by him
elsewhere, and may be found in his published
poems: —

> . . . .
> " Steps have their various meanings — who can hear
> The long, slow tread, deliberate and clear,
> The boot that creaks and gloats on every stair,
> And the firm knock which says, 'I know you're there,'
> Nor quake at portents which so oft before
> Have been the heralds of the ten-inch bore ?
>
> " He enters, and he sits, as crowners sit,
> On the dead bodies of our time and wit ;
> Hopes that no plan of yours he comes to balk,
> And grinds the hurdy-gurdy of his talk
> In steady circles, meaningless and flat
> As the broad brim that rounds a bishop's hat.
> Nature, didst thou endow him with a voice,
> As mothers give great drums to little boys,
> To teach us sadly how much outward din
> Is based on bland vacuity within ?
> . . . .
>   " Who, untouched, could leave
> Those Hebrew songs that triumph, trust, or grieve ?
> Verses that smite the soul as with a sword,

And open all the abysses with a word ?
How many a soul have David's tears washed white,
His wings borne upward to the Source of light !
How many his triumph nerved with martyr-will,
His faith from turmoil led to waters still !
They were his songs that rose to heaven before
The surge of steel broke wild o'er Marston Moor,
When rough-shod workmen in their sober gear
Rode down in dust the long-haired cavalier ;
With these once more the Mayflower's cabin rang,
From men who trusted in the God they sang,
And Plymouth heard them, poured on bended knees,
From wild cathedrals arched with centuried trees.
They were grim men, unlovely — yes, but great —
Who prayed around the cradle of our State.
Small room for light and sentimental strains
In those lean men with empires in their brains,
Who their young Israel saw in vision clasp
The mane of either sea with taming grasp;
Who pitched a state as other men pitch tents,
And led the march of time to great events.

" O strange new world, that yet wast never young,
Whose youth from thee by tyrannous need was wrung,
Brown foundling of the forests, with gaunt eyes,
Orphan and heir of all the centuries,
Who on thy baby leaf-bed in the wood
Grew'st frugal plotting for to-morrow's food;
And thou, dear Bay State, mother of us all,
Forget not in new cares thine ancient call !

"Though all things else should perish in the sod,
Hold with firm clutch thy Pilgrim faith in God,
And the calm courage that deemed all things light
Whene'er the inward voice said, ' *This is right!* '
If for the children there should come a time
Like that which tried the fathers' faith sublime
(Which God avert !), if Tyranny should strive
On limbs New-England-made to lock her gyve,
Let Kansas answer from her reddened fields,
'' T is bastard, and not Pilgrim blood, that yields ! ' "

Until his death, his well-earned reputation as a

public speaker made constant calls on him for service in such directions. But no lover of Lowell will suppose that lecturing to large audiences or to small was much more than an " avocation " with him. The " Fable for Critics," the " Biglow Papers," and other books belong to years when he was hard at work as a college professor. His contributions to the journals which were influential in reform still continued, though not so frequent as before.

CHAPTER IX

THE happiness of Lowell's happy home was shattered by the death of his wife, October 27, 1853. He spent the summer of the next year at Beverly, on the seashore of Massachusetts, in the summer of 1855 went again to Europe, and returned in 1856. He at once resumed his residence at Cambridge, and, with the opening term of the autumn, entered heartily and energetically on his duty as " Smith Professor."

For there was once a gentleman named Abiel Smith. He is wholly unknown to fame. But I wish at this late moment to express the gratitude, hitherto never fitly spoken, of thousands upon thousands of those whom he has blessed. He left to Harvard College, as early as 1815, the foundation for the Smith Professorship of the Modern Languages.

He was himself a graduate of Harvard College in the year 1764, " went into business," as our New England phrase has it, and became rich, as that word was used in those early days. He is spoken of by Mr. Quincy as a man " of strong sense and steady purpose, guiding his life by his own convictions of duty, with little esteem for popular opinion or posthumous fame ; scrupulously just and honest ; practicing habits of frugality less from regard to wealth than out of respect to the example."

It is the fashion to laugh at the name of Smith ; but it must be confessed that a good many people who have had to go through life under that banner have done the world good service.

> " Jones teach him modesty and Greek,
>   Smith how to think, Burke how to speak."

This is the Smith couplet in the fine account of the Beefsteak Club.   If Abiel Smith never did as much thinking as Adam, he must, all the same, be remembered as a benefactor.   He certainly never did so much harm as Adam Smith has done, if he has not done more good.

I am apt to think that this modest man was the first person in the English-speaking world to recognize the value of the systematic study of the modern languages in any university of England or America. A smattering of French was taught at our Cambridge as early as 1780, and Jefferson studied some French at William and Mary's at about the same time.   Charles Bellini was made Professor of the Modern Languages there in 1781.   This recognition of the foreign languages of civilization was due probably to the Philistine fact that we were the allies of a Bourbon king.

The first professor under this Smith foundation was George Ticknor, a graduate of Dartmouth College of the year 1807, now known everywhere in the world of letters by his history of Spanish literature. I found this book the working book of reference in the Royal Library at Madrid — which, by the way, is the most elegant working public library I ever saw. Ticknor was professor from 1820 to 1835. Henry Wadsworth Longfellow was his immediate successor, and, when Longfellow resigned in 1854, Lowell was appointed to succeed him. This is a brilliant series, the honors of which have been well sustained since Lowell died.

I have seen it somewhere said that Lowell disliked the work of a college professor. In a way, I suppose this statement may be literally true. That is to say, like other men who know how to work hard, it was not agreeable to him to be called off at a particular hour to do a particular thing for a particular length of time, and so far to interrupt the regular line of his study or thought for the day. But he was not a fool, and he accepted the universe frankly. So that, if it were his duty to walk down from Elmwood to the college and see how a particular class was getting on in Spanish, or how the particular teacher handled the beginners in French, he could do that as well as another. He would scold, in his funny way, about such interruption of his more interesting work, — so do the rest of us, — but if the thing were to be done, he did it. I say this at the beginning of what I want to say about his position at Cambridge as a teacher.

In describing the four years between 1834 and 1838, the years of his undergraduate life, I tried to give some idea of what an American college was in those prehistoric times. Simply, it was a somewhat enlarged country " academy." The wonder was that the boys did not study in the rooms in which they recited, as they would have done in such an academy. That would have completed the resemblance to such a school. The distinction that you studied your lesson in your own room and recited it in another building was the principal distinction between your work at the Boston Latin School, or Leicester Academy, and the work which you did in college. Thus, you were told that your lesson was to be eighty lines of Euripides's "Hecuba." You sat down at your task in the evening, looked out the words and found out how to read it, you went down the next day and recited it, and went back again. That was all which Hecuba was to you, or you to Hecuba. I can conceive of nothing more dull.

Governor Everett once said very well that a school was a place where you recited a lesson which somebody outside had taught you. This was quite true in those days. For one, as I ought to have said in an earlier chapter, I had but four teachers in college, — Channing, Longfellow, Peirce, and Bachi. The rest heard me recite but taught me nothing.

In the twenty years between 1834 and 1855, the change had begun at Cambridge which has made of the college of to-day an entirely different place, with entirely different customs and traditions. It was in a great address delivered by Dr. Hedge at the Phi Beta Kappa in 1840 that the first visible token of this change appeared before the somewhat startled gaze of corporation, overseers, and graduates. Dr. Hedge said squarely then that this sort of schoolboy work could not long continue in a civilized country like ours, and that everybody must go to work to lift the college to a higher grade.

I think he thought that the age of undergraduates was to be greater than it was before. I think we all thought so. I am told, however, now, that the experience of the years since that time has not justified this supposition. I believe that the average of the age of the boys in the college classes is but a few months older than it proved to be then. But I am disposed to think that in the prehistoric days there came in more grown men — rather sporadic instances, indeed, but still a good many of them — and that the presence of these grown men in the classes raised the statistics of average of those periods. If two or three queer antediluvian fellows of thirty-five came into the midst of a class of fifty boys of sixteen, why, they screwed up the average age by several months. I do not understand that such sporadic cases occur very often now. Anyway, the doctrine of Dr. Hedge's address is that the college shall open its doors to teach what it can teach; that there shall be a chance for the teachers themselves to be learning something in the lines of original research, and that every encouragement shall be given to the learner to follow the " bent of his genius," as Mr. Emerson says somewhere, and that he shall not be made to do certain things because somebody else has done them.

The line of Presidents of short periods, which followed, was a line of men not disinclined to these larger views. Neither Dr. Sparks, nor Dr. Felton,

nor Dr. Hill had a long enough term of office to
do much in the direction in which President Eliot
has so boldly stepped forward. But they were not
averse to enlarging the life of the University. Certainly Lowell was in sympathy with any such endeavor.

The Smith professorship, as I have intimated,
gave opportunity for a pretty wide range of duty on
the part of the professor. He had, indeed, a wider
range than any other professor had in any other
department. He was virtually responsible, as a su-
perintendent, for the verbal instruction about nom-
inative cases and verbs and *der* and *die* and *das*,
which had to be given, if young men were to know
anything about the literature of the languages
taught. These languages were French, German,
Italian, Spanish, and Portuguese. But the real detail of the instruction in these languages was given
by people who were called assistant professors or instructors; and the professor himself, so far as he
had a function of his own, was a lecturer on important themes bearing on the literary life of the last
two cr three centuries. As early as Longfellow's
day, he delivered in college a series of lectures on
Dante, which embodied much of what one finds in
the notes to his translation of the poet. Lowell
began his course by reading to the students the
lectures which he had delivered in Boston. In the
twenty years of his active professorship he delivered
to them several courses of similar lectures.

If you talk with any of the men now on the stage
who were with him in college, you find that they

associate him especially with these brilliant lectures
which students liked to attend. But you find much
more than this. Those who knew him at all, and
who took any interest in the line of study to which
he was committed, remember him from their personal intimacies with him. I was myself much interested, in the years between 1866 and 1870, in the
college fortunes of Frederick Wadsworth Loring, a
young fellow who died, too soon as it seemed, only
a year after he graduated. He has left behind quite
enough to justify those of us who remember him in
what we say of his remarkable promise. I saw that
boy when he was seven years old, sitting on a foot-
stool at his mother's feet, reading Shakespeare
eagerly. I said to her, "Take care! Pray take
care!" And she said to me, with an expression
which I have never forgotten, "Oh, we know the
danger, and I think we are careful!" And they
were. She died, alas! in the year 1859. He was,
so to speak, pitchforked into college, and found
himself there, with his passionate enthusiasm for literature and poetry, after very hard and uncomfort-
able discipline at a poor country academy. And at
Cambridge, as in Lowell's time, there was chapel
which must be attended, there was this and that
which must be learned, and so-and-so which must
be done. And here was Loring, wild about the
majestic achievements of the great poets. He was
utterly indifferent as to the systems of Ptolemy or
of Newton; and the world might have rolled backward for five years without his caring. Yet must is
must, and he had to pretend to study mathematics.

What would have happened to the dear boy but for the existence of two men, I do not know; but, fortunately for him and for those who loved him, here was Lowell at the head of the department of modern languages, and Elbridge Jefferson Cutler at the head of the English subdivision. And, after four years of Loring's college life, which was of value to him that no man can pretend to describe, he graduated. I think, indeed, that they gave him a poem at Commencement. I have never forgotten that when I was at the " spread " in Holworthy, where Loring modestly entertained his friends on Class Day, I met Cutler, and I said to him, " Well, Cutler, you have got Fred through." " Yes," he said, " we have dragged him through by the hair of his head."

" We " meant Lowell and himself. They were perfectly determined that this brilliant young poet should get what could be got out of the university. They were perfectly determined that no waywardness of his own should break up the regular course of life which offered such promise. And if I told some of the stories of the affectionate way in which those two distinguished men cared for the life of this distinguished boy, it would be a story out of which some one who knew how to hold a pen could make a fascinating romance or drama. It would, perhaps, do something to remove the preposterous and ridiculous impression of the more foolish undergraduate that " the faculty " hates him.

On the catalogue Mr. Lowell's position as Smith Professor covers thirty years. In 1886 he resigned to be appointed " Professor Emeritus," and so his

name remains on the college catalogue until his
death. In 1865 he had the welcome relief of the
appointment of Mr. Cutler as an assistant. The department was gradually enlarged with the enlarge-
ment of the college, but for thirty years it was
under Mr. Lowell's general administration, excepting during his journeys in Europe and his diplomatic residence in Madrid and in London.

This boy of 1838 left college to try the experiments of life, not really knowing what life had for
him. In the seventeen years between 1838 and
1855 he had been in Europe two or three times,
and, as the reader knows, he had spent a part of one
winter in Philadelphia. But Cambridge had been
his home most of the time, and he had seen step by
step the changes which made this "academy" or
"seminary" into a university. Some of the officers still remained to whom he had recited when in
college.

Josiah Quincy had been succeeded as President
by Edward Everett, and Jared Sparks, and James
Walker, the last of whom was now the President.

Dr. Walker's name may not be universally known
among students in all parts of this country, especially by men of those religious schools who made
it a duty to brand him and the men of his communion as infidels. But it is safe to say that no
man was in college during the twenty-two years in
which he was professor and president who does not
remember him with gratitude and speak of him with
enthusiasm. From 1838 to 1853 he was the Professor of Natural Religion and Moral Philosophy.

He lectured on these subjects in the Lowell Institute. He often preached in the college pulpit, and to this day, when you meet any of his old hearers, you will find that they hark back to him and what he said to them with distinct memory of the lessons, practical and profound, which he enforced.

Not long before the close of his life he supplied for one winter the pulpit of a church a little away from the centre of Boston. Every Sunday saw a procession of his old pupils, twenty years older, perhaps, than they were as undergraduates, who gladly seized this occasion to profit by the wisdom of their old counselor.

Cornelius Conway Felton, to whom I have already referred in speaking of the Mutual Admiration Society, succeeded Dr. Walker. He had been Greek Professor when Lowell was an undergraduate. His successor, Dr. Thomas Hill, graduated five years after Lowell.

Of his old professors Lowell found in office Lovering and Benjamin Peirce. There were one or two instructors in the modern languages who had survived the interval, but for the rest his coadjutors had been appointed since his graduation.

The college had been taking on her larger methods in those seventeen years, and during what was left of his life he saw and assisted in other changes larger yet. From the beginning he cut red tape or threw it away. He cultivated close acquaintance with the young men whom he met in his classes, and he and the men of his type have done much to bring about interest and sympathy between teacher

CORNELIUS CONWAY FELTON

and taught, such as was hardly dreamed of in Cambridge in the first half of the century. The two volumes of his published letters give a charming view of his relations with Longfellow, Norton, Cutler, and other professors of his time, and, indeed, of the cordial social life of Cambridge. Of these gentlemen I have something I should like to say in another paper of this series. But this is the better place to allude to the young poet, Hugh Clough, who is alluded to in Lowell's correspondence with his associates in Cambridge. Clough came to Cambridge, as I have always supposed, in the real hope of adapting himself to American life, or life in a republic, where "I am as good as the other fellow, and the other fellow is as good as I." Alas and alas! how many of us have seen Englishmen who tried this great experiment, who made the great emigration, and then were obliged to go back to the leeks of Egypt! I do not know that it was so with Clough, but I think it was.

People who remember his "Bothie of Tober-na-Vuolich" (and they are not so many as there should be) will recollect that that charming poem closes as white handkerchiefs are waved in an adieu when the English steamer leaves her dock and sails with the hero and heroine for Australia — "a brave new land," without fuss and without feathers, without feudalism and the follies of feudalism; a land of freedom.

"Five hundred pounds in pocket, with books, and two or three pictures,
  Tool-box, plow, and the rest, they rounded the sphere to New Zealand. . . .

"There hath he farmstead and land, and fields of corn and flax
    fields,
  And the Antipodes too have a Bothie of Tober-na-Vuolich."

And other readers will remember that, for nearly
a generation, more than half the English novels
which turned out well, ended thus, in a flourish of
trumpets in which anybody who was good for anything went away from England. Even Carlyle's
Chartism had nothing better to propose than that
England should send away the people she did not
know how to take care of at home. Among them
Clough came, but apparently he was too old. He
went back to England, and, I think, accepted a
government office — not, perhaps, inspector of slate-
pencils, but something not more edifying. He died
in 1862, in Florence.

He was a charming poet, and I cannot but think
a charming companion. I always think of him as a
bishop "in partibus," a bishop without a mitre or
a see. For Mr. Emerson told me an interesting
story of Clough. He was one of a cluster of young
men who had taken great delight in Emerson, on
his visit in 1848 in England. When that visit was
over, and Mr. Emerson sailed for America on his
return, Clough accompanied him to Liverpool and
bade him good-by on the deck of the steamer. As
they walked up and down the deck together, Clough
said sadly, "What shall we do without you?
Think where we are. Carlyle has led us all out
into the desert, and he has left us there" — a remark which was exactly true. Emerson said in
reply that very many of the fine young men in

England had said this to him as he went up and down in his journeyings there. "And I put my hand upon his head as we walked, and I said, 'Clough, I consecrate you Bishop of all England. It shall be your part to go up and down through the desert to find out these wanderers and to lead them into the promised land.'"

I do not know, but I am afraid that Clough never thought himself in the promised land, nor scarcely upon any Pisgah looking down upon it. But I tell the story, as showing how highly Emerson thought of Clough as far back as 1849.

As I have said, Lowell succeeded Longfellow, who had come to Cambridge when Lowell was a sophomore; and Lowell, like every one else who worked under Longfellow, was always grateful to him. Longfellow began, all too early, the habit of speaking of himself as an old man. But the published volumes of his own life show how diligent and active he was, and that he considered his relief from the daily work of his professorship as simply an opportunity for wider work in literature.

By his boundless liberality to every child of sorrow he had made Cambridge the Mecca of a polyglot pilgrimage in which any European exiles who could read or write came of course to the Craigie House to ask for his patronage and assistance. With Mr. Lowell's arrival there were, I think, no fewer of such visitors at the Craigie House; but by the law of the instrument they found their way by the pleasant shady walk which leads from Longfellow's home to Elmwood and Mount Auburn.

I remember among these an accomplished gentleman, who worked in America in the anti-slavery
cause, in ante-bellum days. He always was grateful to Longfellow for his assistance to him, which
came at a time when it was most needed. Heinrich
von Hutten was a lineal descendant, I think, of
Ulrich von Hutten, the poet of the Reformation.
He came to this country in the suite of Kossuth,
who ought, perhaps, to have been spoken of elsewhere in this series. Von Hutten gave his life and
strength, and perhaps his blood, to the Hungarian
cause. After his arrival here he was employed by
a publishing firm to translate Mrs. Stowe's " Uncle
Tom's Cabin " into the German language. After
he had begun, there was a terror lest a rival translation should be finished before his, and the good
Von Hutten worked day and night — too much,
alas ! by night — in completing the work assigned
to him. The story always reminds me of Milton's
sonnet,

> " What sustains me, dost thou ask ?
> The conscience, friend, to have lost them overplied
> In Liberty's defense, my noble task,"

for he really lost his eyes in the cause of freedom.
   Longfellow was kind to him, Lowell was kind to
him, and, indeed, he was a man who deserved to
have friends everywhere. When I was in Europe
in 1873, I was glad to hear that the good Von
Hutten was living again in the castle of his ancestors upon the Danube River. It was one of the
minor misfortunes of my life that I was not able to
accept his invitation to visit him there.

ELMWOOD

As I have said, it has been intimated that Lowell
chafed under the regular requisitions of the duties
of a professor. And, as I have said, most men do
chafe a little when they find that on a given day
they are expected to do a given thing where they
want to do something else. It must be discoura-
ging to have a class of boys around you to whom a
lesson is simply a bore, and to know that you will
hear, at twenty-seven minutes after eleven, the same
stupid mistake which you heard made at twenty-six
minutes after eleven, three hundred and sixty-five
days ago. In his private letters there is occasionally an expression, sometimes serious and sometimes
gay, of the dislike of the necessary slavery which
follows on such work. But he had accepted it, for
better for worse, and went through with it loyally.
He liked the intercourse which his work gave him
with young men of promise, and availed himself
gladly of every opportunity to make the intercourse
of advantage to them. In a charming and suggestive paper by Professor Barrett Wendell, which was
published in "Scribner's" immediately after Lowell's death, there is such detail as only a college professor could write of some of the methods and habits
in which Lowell grew into a friendly intimacy with
his pupils. He assigned one evening in a week
when they might call to see him, and he was so
cordial then that they took the impression that he
liked to see them, and would go up on any evening
when they chose. I am favored with the private
journal of one of these pupils, in which are many
anecdotes, some even pathetic, of the cordial inter-

course he had with them.   Professor Wendell gives
a valuable account of his own experience with Lowell.   He had never studied any Italian, and yet he
boldly resolved that he would ask Lowell's permis-
sion to attend his lectures on Dante, though he had
no knowledge of the Italian language.   Lowell was
pleased, perhaps was interested in seeing what so
bright a boy would do under such circumstances;
and the result of this was, as Mr. Wendell says,
"at the end of a month I could read Dante better
than I ever learned to read Greek or Latin or German."   Remember this, gentlemen who are taking
nine years to teach a boy to read Latin; and reflect
that Mr. Wendell reads his Latin as well as the best
of you.

I think the reader may indulge me in a little
excursus when I say a few words seriously to the
undergraduates of to-day with regard to this form
of cordial intercourse between them and their professors.   We used to say, when I was in college,
that we wished the professors would treat us as gentlemen.   The wish is a very natural one.   I have
had many classes myself in the fifty or sixty years
which have followed, and I have always tried to live
up to that undergraduate theory.   I have treated
my pupils as if they wanted to learn and were gentlemen, and their honor could be relied upon.   Looking back on it, I think I should say that about half
of them have met me more than halfway.   But —
and here lies the warning which I wish to give to
undergraduates — the other half have taken an ell
where I gave an inch.   Because I did not crowd

them they did nothing; they considered me a
"soft" person, and my course a "soft" course. In
other words, they shirked, simply because I did not
treat them with the methods of a low-grade gram-
mar-school.

Young gentlemen, then, ought to consider how
far they are themselves responsible for any supposed
harshness or mechanical habit on the part of the
gentlemen who really know more than they do, and
who are willing to trust them in their work. I had
the honor last spring of being appointed as one of
the judges of some prose exercises in one of our
older colleges. I was proud and glad to give the
time which the examination of these exercises required. What did I find? I found, of three different papers submitted to me in competition on the
same subject, that all the writers had stolen, from
reviews which they supposed would not be known,
long passages, and copied them as their own. In
this particular case, it happened that the three writers were so ignorant of the literature of the last half-
century that they copied the same passage, hoping
that the judges of their exercises would be ignorant
enough to be deceived. Is it not rather hard to be
told that you are to "treat as gentlemen" black-
guards like these, who are willing to tell lies for so
petty a purpose as was involved in this endeavor?
I should say that the Greek-letter societies have it
in their power to do a good deal to tone up the
undergraduate conscience in such affairs.

To return to Lowell: He was quite beyond and
above confining himself to the requisitions of his

profession. As an instance of his generosity in this way, in the winter of 1865 he offered to the divinity students to come round to them and lecture familiarly to them on the mediæval idea of hell as it may be gathered from Dante. This was no part of the business of his chair. He volunteered for it as the reader of these lines might offer to take a class in a Sunday-school. I remember that some of the students took a notion that he pinched himself by his generous help to those whom he thought in need. One of his pupils told me that Lowell offered him a Christmas present of valuable books, under the pretext that he was thinning out his book-shelves. " I declined them," said my friend, " simply from the feeling that he could not afford to give them. I need not say," he says, " that I am sorry for this now."

I am favored by Mr. Robert Lincoln, who was fortunate enough to be one of his pupils, with the following memoranda of the impression which he made upon them : —

DEAR DOCTOR HALE, — My only association with Mr. Lowell in college was as a member of a small class who " went through " Dante under his supervision. Our duty was to prepare ourselves to translate the text, and Mr. Lowell heard our blunderings with a wonderful patience, and rewarded us with delightful talks on matters suggested in the poem; but we had no set lecture. My experience (that is, at Harvard), therefore, only permits me to speak of him as a professor in the recitation-room. In that

relation his erudition, humor, and kindness made
me, and I am sure all my associates, enjoy the hour
with him as we did no other college exercise. I can
sincerely say that it is one of my most highly cher-
ished experiences. With us he was always conver-
sational, and flattered us and gained us by an
assumption that what interested him interested us.
When now I take up my Dante, Mr. Lowell seems
to be with me. . . .

Always sincerely yours,

Robert T. Lincoln.

It will be seen that the impression made on Mr.
Lincoln, and his memories of Lowell, are similar to
those of Mr. Wendell.

From the journal to which I have referred I copy
the following passages: —

"June 12, 1865, I went to look at the scenery
from Mount Auburn tower. Returning, I found
the serene possessor of Elmwood in good spirits, ate
a Graham biscuit and drank some delicious milk
with him and his wife, then enjoyed a very pleasant
conversation. He read some of Shakespeare's sonnets, to make me think better of them, and succeeded. His noble old dog Argus had been poisoned,
and in Argus's place he had a young Newfoundland
pup which he called Bessie, as black Aggy Green,
on Port Royal Island, named her pet sow! He gave
me a very welcome copy of Macaulay's essays and
poems, and the little visit was another oasis in
school life's dearth of home sociability. Mabel, his
only child, was not there at supper, but came home

some time after: 'Salute your progenitor!' and
the answer was a daughter's kiss.

"In September, 1865, he offered to conduct the
divinity students into Dante's conception of hell,
and as far out as time would allow. He read the
first canto through for introduction, and gave me
the second for our first trial. I went, because I
wanted to become inured, lest I might have to conduct somebody else. He had too many other duties,
was somewhat unwell, cut the Dante for both days
of a week three or four times, some of the readers
were not Italian enough to read easily, and on December 13 he gave us up as a lost tribe of the race
of Adam. January 19, 1866, I was his guest again,
clear even of the central frozen bolgia. After dinner he gave me a card to Longfellow, whom I found
about four o'clock at his dinner."

The same accurate critic writes: —

"In Lowell's college work the weakest part was
his class teaching. While no teacher in the university was more willing to help his boys, his habit of
doing most of the reading, when a boy labored,
with friction, breaking right into his reading, was
not agreeable to the boy. But even in that he at
least had the courage of mastery, and never shirked
the hard passages. His corrections and remarks
were often lost from the want of clearness and
open-mouthed carefulness of articulation. When he
spoke in public he always made himself heard; but
to a small, almost private class, speaking without
effort, his modest stillness and his smothering mus-
tache would make us wish that men's hair had been

forbidden to grow forward of the corner of their mouths."

I must postpone other references to Mr. Lowell's life with his students to the next chapter, which will speak of him in his relations to the civil war, which followed so soon after his appointment at Cambridge. His home at Cambridge for much of the first two years of his professorship had been with Dr. and Mrs. Howe, in Kirkland Street. In September, 1857, he was able to return to Elmwood and reëstablish family life, after his fortunate and happy marriage to Miss Frances Dunlap.

Every person who has had any experience in teaching knows that the great danger to a school-master or a professor is that he shall know but little of what passes outside his own cocoon. There is an old satirical fling which says that a schoolmaster is a man who does not take the voyage of life him-self, but stands on the gangway of the steamer to pass those along who are going to take it. This is not true, but it has just foundation enough to give point to the satire, and to give suggestion to those who are in danger.

The danger is that a man shall think that half the world is contained in the ring-fence which in-closes the territory where they hear his academy bell. Can you conceive of a better antidote for his sweet poison, or a better rescue from his dangers, than the occupation of an editor? Mr. Lowell, in handling the "North American" and the "Atlan-tic," had to see that there were people quite as much interested in life as he, who lived in Texas and in Washington Territory and in the Sandwich Islands and in New Zealand. He did not open a morning's mail but it taught him that the world, while it is a very small place, is a small place which has some very large conditions. He was that sort of a man that his nature could never have been petty or provincial; but the avocations which editorial life brought him would of themselves have made him cosmopolitan.

CHAPTER X

LOWELL'S EXPERIENCE AS AN EDITOR

LOWELL'S whole life was a literary life, from the days of the "Boston Miscellany" and of the "Pioneer." And I am well aware that these notes will be read with a certain special interest by young people who are asking themselves whether literature, as such, offers "a career" to those who are entering upon life.

It required much more resolution to determine on such a career in America in 1841 than it does now. I will attempt, therefore, in this paper, to bring together such illustrations of Lowell's life as a man of letters as we may have room for, which do not specially connect themselves with the political history of the times, or with his special work as a professor in Harvard College.

In an earlier chapter I have already printed some of the pathetic memoranda which show how modestly his career began. Knowing as we do that, before he was fifty years old, this man was to rank as one of the first poets of his time, is it not pathetic to find him writing to his nearest friend to ask whether it is probable that three hundred copies of his poems can be sold?

It happened, as also has appeared in that chapter,

that it was the periodical press which gave the
means of physical support to the young man who
was attempting this venture. In the same chapter
I cited what is the really funny criticism of Willis,
if he made it, — when he says that a man of genius
may not be a good editor. As it happened, Lowell
devoted much of his after life to the steady business
of editing periodicals. I mean by this, not simply
the general oversight of the plan of the journal
for which he was responsible, but that diligent and
tedious daily work, whether of reading manuscripts,
of correcting and improving them, of correspondence
with writers, and of hourly intimacy with publishers,
which makes at once the drudgery and the pleasure
of real editorial life. I observe that most young
men and women who think they want to be " connected with the press " suppose that such a connection will simply compel them to go to the theatre
every night, and to read agreeable novels and magazines all day. I have had a good deal to do with
editorial life myself, and I have not found that this
general impression regarding it is correct. Certainly
Lowell never " got round to it." He worked with
steadfast diligence. He says in one place that he
worked more than fifteen hours, on an average,
every day. This means that he really read the
manuscripts which he had in hand, that he really
looked over the range of the world's business to see
what he wanted, and that he tried to engage such
authors as were best fitted for special work in the
journal for which he was engaged. His acquaintance with men and women became larger and larger

as he did this, and there is many a pretty story of
the encouragement which he gave to young writers
at the very beginning of their career.

Thus, there was a joke afterwards between him
and Mr. Aldrich. When Aldrich, somewhat tim-
idly, sent his first poem to the "Atlantic," Lowell
at once recognized its worth, and sent to him the
most cordial thanks. Many years after, Aldrich
found himself, in turn, editor of the "Atlantic."
Lowell, then at the height of his reputation, sent a
poem to the magazine. Aldrich had the fun to
copy, in acknowledging the manuscript, the very
note which Lowell wrote to him, most kindly, twenty
years before, in which he recognized the value of
his first contribution. Lowell came round to the
office at once, and told Aldrich that he had almost
determined him " to adopt a literary career."

As the reader knows, Lowell edited the " Pioneer " for its short existence of three months.

In the summer of 1846 he agreed to write once a
week, in prose or in poetry, for the " Anti-Slavery
Standard," the best of the anti-slavery journals. He
was called a corresponding editor. The paper was
edited by the masterly hand of Mr. Sidney Gay,
afterwards the editor of the " Popular History."

Mr. Lawrence Lowell, in his interesting memoir
of the poet's life, calls the few years from 1846 to
1850 the most active and the most happy of his life.
" His happiness was, indeed, broken by the death
of little Blanche, in March, 1847 ; but a new joy
came to him in the birth of another daughter, Rose,
toward the close of the year. Both grief and joy,

however, seem to have stimulated his poetic feeling,
and poems such as 'The First Snowfall' and 'The
Changeling' show the ecstasy to which they brought
his nature.   During all this period he wrote inces-
santly, sometimes about public affairs, sometimes
from a purely poetic impulse, with no direct relation
to the great struggle in which he was engaged, but
almost always with a stern sense of his mission as a
prophet and a seer.   His character no less than his
poetic feeling had deepened and strengthened, and
poems like 'The Present Crisis' attest the full
maturity of his powers."

When Phillips & Sampson established the "Atlantic Monthly," in the autumn of 1857, he was its
first regular editor; and there are some very nice
letters of his in which he speaks of the somewhat
sudden change in the methods of his daily life which
come in as he walks along the river-bank from Elmwood and takes the street-car to the office in Boston.
If there were room, I could hardly print anything
more interesting than specimens of the notes which
he wrote to authors.   They give a very pretty picture of the watchful interest which he took in each
individual number of the "Atlantic."   It is as the
mother of a large family might not let her children
go to a Christmas party without seeing that the
hands of each one were perfectly clean, and that the
collar of each one was prettier and neater than the
others'.   I think I may say that, in a somewhat
varied experience in such matters, I have known no
editor who had so close a watchful eye on the detail
of the work of his journal.

JAMES T. FIELDS

This connection with the "Atlantic" lasted for four years, when James T. Fields, the prince among editors, took his place. In the year 1863, in company with his very dear friend Mr. Charles Eliot Norton, he became the editor of the "North American Review." What this meant appears from the fact that between the years 1863 and 1877 he wrote thirty-four "articles" for the "North American," besides as many more of what, in the language of that day, were called "critical notices." In the "Atlantic Monthly," between the years 1857 and 1877, he wrote one hundred and sixteen articles, prose or poetry.

There are, as I have intimated, a great many men now prominent among our men of letters who recollect Lowell gratefully as being the Beatrice who first welcomed them into this Paradise. Without attempting to name half of them, I will say that Mr. Howells, whom he welcomes so cordially in a letter which is to be found in Mr. Norton's collection, and Mr. Aldrich, to whom I referred just now, both afterwards became editors of the "Atlantic" themselves. In their time they have passed on the welcome which the prince of American poets gave to both of them. And each of them inherited in turn the traditions of the office, as he established them.

The establishment of the "Atlantic Monthly" in the autumn of 1857 proved so fortunate an era in the history of the native literature of America that I may safely give to it a few sentences in these memorials. Lowell's connection with that magazine enlarged very widely the circle of his friends and the range of his life.

It was, then, two or three years since the little Eden of Boston bookselling had been disturbed in its somnolence to a sudden "new departure," if we may borrow an admirable phrase from the forgotten times when we had a mercantile marine. This "new departure" was the movement, as of a stork among a world of frogs, instituted by Phillips & Sampson, a new-born firm among booksellers.

The publishing business in Boston felt the wave of their impetuosity. It can hardly be said that the old houses waked from the decorous sleep of many years. But this new publishing house, with manners and customs wholly unknown before, suddenly appeared, to the dumb amazement of the old stand-bys, and to the delight and amusement of all young America, in the East.

Boston had never earned for itself its distinct position as one of the publishing centres of America. It had inherited that position without earning it. Harvard College, the Boston Athenæum, the American Academy, the Massachusetts Historical Society, the New England system of lectures, and the great free school system, which gave a liberal education to any boy who would take it, — these, all together, created a circle of authors. They created the "Monthly Anthology," the "North American Review," and the "Christian Examiner." Such men as Bancroft, Prescott, Hildreth, Sparks, the Everetts, Hawthorne, Emerson, and now Lowell, came forward with books which had to be published. The loyalty of the Boston lawyers to their business, of the doctors to theirs, and of the ministers to theirs, had made it necessary that there should be printers and shops where books could be bought and sold. So the importers of English books had become, in a languid way, the publishers of books.

But they did not want to publish them. They did not expect to make money by publishing them. They did not know anything about them. Alexander Everett used to say that a bookseller was the only tradesman who knew nothing about the wares he sold. Of the Boston trade in those prehistoric days this was substantially true. But, in truth, there was not much publishing, excepting the issue of some law books and a few medical books. Hilliard & Gray, and Crocker & Brewster, attended to these affairs and cared little for any others.

Any one of the old firms regarded an author with a manuscript much as a dealer in Russian sail-cloth might regard a lady who should come into his counting-room and ask him to make her a linen handkerchief.

All of a sudden, as a wave of water might sweep over a thick, rotten ice-floe in one of Nansen's summers, a marvelous inundation swept over this decorous imbecility. That is to say, two young men formed a "publishing firm." They did not want to import books. They wanted to make them and to sell them.

More simply speaking, "Phillips & Sampson" appeared about the year 1843. Charles Sampson (a young man when he died in 1858) used to say

that he had peddled molasses candy from a tin
waiter on holidays, when he was a boy. Moses
Dresser Phillips had been brought up to the retail
book trade in Worcester, in the shop of Clarendon
Harris, who succeeded Isaiah Thomas, the publisher
of the first American Bible. I do not know how
these young fellows first met each other. But it
was they who taught the drowsy chiefs of the little
Boston book-shops the great lesson that in a nation which had taught thirty million people how to
read, there were more than five hundred people
who wanted to read Emerson's essays or Macaulay's
history.

Emerson, as has been said, had never received
one cent from the publication of his essays, when
Phillips & Sampson, about 1850, published "English Traits" for him. Mr. Phillips was by marriage connected with Emerson's family, and had
persuaded him to leave James Monroe and give the
new book to the younger firm, now well established
in business.

But this new firm meant to make books which
everybody must buy, and to sell them where anybody could read. They did not pretend to retail
books, any more than the Pacific Mills pretend to sell
to a good housewife the material for a shirt or a sheet.
They did mean to make them and to sell them to
the retailers. So far as the nation at large went, or
a wholesale trade with dealers anywhere, they had
hardly any rivals in Boston. Opposite them was
the shop of Ticknor & Fields. The young, wide-
awake James T. Fields, now so well known by his

MOSES DRESSER PHILLIPS

charming reminiscences and other essays, had entered that shop, as "youngest boy," in the later
thirties. His broad and intelligent foresight was
beginning to bear fruit. But Allen & Ticknor can
hardly be numbered among publishers, and Ticknor
& Fields did not exist as a firm until Cummings &
Hilliard had become Hilliard & Gray. This firm
published law books and medical books. Crocker
& Brewster, successors to Governor Armstrong, imported and sold theological books. I bought my
Hebrew Bible and my Gesenius's Lexicon from
them in 1839. But, if a man wanted one of these
firms to publish a book for him, why, they would
have told him that he must pay for his plates and
his printing. Thus Mr. Bancroft, fortunately for
himself, owned the plates and the printed copies of
his own History from 1833 until he died.

Charles Sampson and Moses Dresser Phillips made
an admirable combination, and the early death of
both of them made a break in the book business of
Boston which it did not easily recover from. These
young men were not satisfied with the gilt-edged
retail "trade" of Boston and Cambridge. They
went far afield with their wares. Mr. Phillips used
to tell with glee the story of their first orders from
San Francisco in the '49 days. " So many hundred
packs of 'Highland' cards, so many of the 'True
Thomas' cards, and so on till the box was nearly
full, and then ' one dozen Bibles.'"

This was seed-corn, he said. And then, in 1852
or 1853, he would read you their last invoices,
as they answered immense orders from California.

"Four hundred Byron's Poems, four hundred
Scott's Poems, one hundred Cowper's Poems," and
so on, in large shipments. And he would say,
"That is the crop that comes from the twelve
Bibles. Such editions of the poets," he would say,
"as you would not have seen in your house, — but,
after all, Cowper is Cowper, and Scott is Scott."

Both these men were resolute to meet the people
halfway. Both of them were Democrats in parti-
san connection, not because they believed in the
heresies of such men as Polk and Dallas, but because they believed in the People. There was
nothing of the white-kid glove, gilt-edged paper,
"u in honour" nonsense about them. Naturally,
such believers as they were regarded as unorthodox
in the trade of that day.

Their great onslaught on decorous publishing
was made when they printed and sold Macaulay's
History for fifty cents a volume at retail.

Such a firm as this won its way up from selling
books at auction, at retail, on winter evenings, to
publishing large editions and placing them everywhere in America. And when the fullness of time
for such an enterprise came, they determined to
publish "The Atlantic Monthly." The plan was
matured in the autumn of 1857. Through the
kindness of a friend, I am able to reprint here Mr.
Phillips's own description, at the time, of a famous
dinner in which the enterprise was first announced
— I ought not to say in public, for this was a private dinner. But I may say that that dinner-party
was the first of a series which the Saturday Club of

Boston has held from that day to this day.   Mr.
Phillips wrote, " I must tell you about a little dinner-
party I gave about two weeks ago.   It would be
proper, perhaps, to state that the origin of it was
a desire to confer with my literary friends on a
somewhat extensive literary project, the particulars
of which I shall reserve till you come.   But to the
party : My invitations included only R. W. Emerson,
H. W. Longfellow, J. R. Lowell, Mr. Motley (the
' Dutch Republic ' man), O. W. Holmes, Mr. Cabot,
and Mr. Underwood, our literary man.   Imagine your
uncle as the head of such a table, with such guests.
The above named were the only ones invited, and
they were all present.   We sat down at three P. M.,
and rose at eight.   The time occupied was longer by
about four hours and thirty minutes than I am in the
habit of consuming in that kind of occupation, but
it was the richest time intellectually by all odds that
I have ever had.   Leaving myself and ' literary man '
out of the group, I think you will agree with me that
it would be difficult to duplicate that number of such
conceded scholarship in the whole country beside.

" Mr. Emerson took the first post of honor at my
right, and Mr. Longfellow the second at my left.
The exact arrangement of the table was as follows :

Mr. Underwood.

Cabot.	Lowell.
Motley.	Holmes.
Longfellow.	Emerson.

Phillips.

" They seemed so well pleased that they adjourned,
and invited me *to meet them* again to-morrow, when

I shall again meet the same persons, with one other
(Whipple, the essayist) added to that brilliant con-
stellation of philosophical, poetical, and historical
talent. Each one is known alike on both sides of
the Atlantic, and is read beyond the limits of the
English language. Though all this is known to
you, you will pardon me for intruding it upon you.
But still I have the vanity to believe that you will
think them the most natural thoughts in the world
to me. Though I say it that should not, it was the
proudest day of my life."

In this letter he does not tell of his own little
speech, made at the launch. But at the time we
all knew of it. He announced the plan of the
magazine by saying, "Mr. Cabot is much wiser than
I am. Dr. Holmes can write funnier verses than I
can. Mr. Motley can write history better than I.
Mr. Emerson is a philosopher and I am not. Mr.
Lowell knows more of the old poets than I." But
after this confession he said, "But none of you
knows the American people as well as I do."

This was the truth, and they knew it was the
truth. The "Atlantic," at that moment, asserted
its true place. It was not "The *Boston* Miscellany;" it was the journal for the nation, which
at that time had no Pacific slope which needed to
be named.

Yet I have guessed that, in the fact that "the
Atlantic States" were then contributing the capital
and the men who were forming the Pacific States,
we find the origin of the very fortunate name
of the magazine. The civilization of the smaller

OLIVER WENDELL HOLMES (1862)

Atlantic basin was beginning to assert itself in that great Pacific basin which implies, when we speak of it, half the surface of the world.   And of such an assertion the " Atlantic " was to be the mouthpiece. But this is my guess only.   I never talked with him about the name, and I do not know who suggested it.   No man then thought of the Philippines.

I always thought that, at the beginning, Mr. Phillips meant to edit the magazine himself.   I do not believe that it occurred to him, before he began, that a magazine office is a place to which every prophet, every poet, and every fool in the land thinks he may send what he chooses to write, and supposes that he is " entitled " to have it read, not to say printed and circulated.   I think he thought he was to ask John, James, and the others, for whom he was publishing books, to send articles fit for the magazine, as Mr. Prescott, for instance, sent a chapter of his " Charles the Fifth."   He did not think that Tom, Dick, or Harry had any " rights " in the business.   Perhaps Mr. Underwood or some one in the office was to read the proofs.

But very soon this simple Arcadian notion vanished.   And very soon Lowell was the working editor of the magazine.

Let me say a word about any presumption that Lowell was a mere figurehead, and that some one else did the work.   Trust me, for I know.   I have worked under many editors, good and bad.   Not one of them understood his business better than Lowell, or worked at its details more faithfully.   I think he hated to read manuscripts as much as any

man of sense does. In those days there was practically no typewriting. I think that, like any man
of sense, he would prefer to write an article than to
read the average " contribution." But he had said
he would do it, and he did it — up to time, so far
as I have seen, careful in detail even to the least
detail, and he had no reason to be ashamed of his
work when he was done.

In those days people of literary aspirations, especially young people, read the English magazines
almost religiously. Indeed, " Blackwood " and
" Frazer " and sometimes the " Dublin University
Magazine" were worth reading. I am afraid that,
for all I have said or implied about the American
or Atlantic basis of the new magazine, the original
cover was, in a way, an imitation of " Blackwood."
The color was, as it is, a sort of tawny brown. It
was more tawny then than it is now. Did it just
suggest the " tawny lion pawing to be free " ? I
do not think Phillips thought of this. Perhaps
Holmes and Lowell did. Where " Blackwood's
Magazine " had and has a medallion head of somebody, we put on the cover of our " maga " the head
of John Winthrop, from the old portrait said to be
by Vandyke, — I do not know why.

Now this was as bad a mistake as the New
Yorkers made in calling their magazine the " Knickerbocker." That is, it gave a local emblem to a
national magazine. John Winthrop was a great
man. But his greatness belonged to Massachusetts,
and not to the nation. West of the Hudson River
there were not a thousand men in the country who
knew anything about him.

But this mistake was not held to. After two years the " Atlantic " had full reason to show that it stood, not for Massachusetts, but for " We, the People of the United States." And the national flag was substituted for the head of a Massachusetts governor. Why it was taken off, I never knew; I doubt if any one else does. One is pleased to see, as this sheet passes the press, that it has appeared again.[1]

In the war the magazine was loyal from hub to tire. Some capital contributions to history are embalmed in it. I remember the late Caleb William Loring's excellent paper on Antietam, a good companion to Dr. Holmes's " Hunt after the Captain."

It may be amusing to preserve one or two reminiscences of the delay with which magazines then appeared, at which writers meekly complained.

The admirable Theodore Winthrop was killed in a miserable outpost skirmish above Hampton. Then, and, alas! not till then, the " Atlantic people " remembered that they had some excellent manuscripts of his, which had been seasoning in the safe, doubtless paid for when they were accepted, but " crowded out" till then. Then they were pushed into type as soon as might be. But death came before the " Atlantic " took the credit, which it deserved, of discovering the author.

I tell this, with some venom, because I myself suffered a little from what Hamlet should have called the pangs of delay of magazine men. I had written for the Ohio canvass of September, 1863, a

---

[1] Alas, to be eclipsed again !

story called "The Man without a Country." It was "rushed through," that it might be in time to defeat Vallandigham in the election of October. And by such swiftness of proofs and revises, unexampled before, it got itself printed in the December number of the same year, when poor Vallandigham had been well beaten and forgotten!

Ah, youngsters of 1898, how little do you know of what you enjoy in these days of "quick proofs, no revises, fast coaches." The true rule for an editor is to send back to each author every manuscript which he has by him, and to trust to February to fill the appetite of March. One does not care to have his eggs too old.

It is to go back a little from the birthday of the "Atlantic" to speak of the first of the "Biglow Papers" ten years before. The series ran for nearly four years.

It was in June, 1846, in face of the almost unanimous hatred of the Mexican War among Massachusetts people, that a regiment was raised in Boston and the neighborhood for that war. Lowell saw a recruiting officer in the street, and was roused to much the sort of wrath which fired the average Boston gentleman in 1773 when he saw a "lobsterback" loafing in the same street with as little reason. Lowell wrote for the "Courier" what he calls "a squib," which was the first of the "Biglow Papers." Mr. Lawrence Lowell reminds us that he did not follow up its success at once. The third paper was published a year and a half after the first. After this the poems of the first series appeared in rapid succession.

If applied with a utilitarian view *(Space this line more)*

Suppose, for example, we shipped it with care

To Sahara's great desert and let it bore there,

~~Let them~~ held one short session and do nothing else,

~~And~~ they 'd fill the whole waste with Artesian wells.

But 'tis time now with pen phonographic to follow

Through some more of his sketches our laughing Apollo:—

"There comes Harry Franco, and, as he draws near,

You find that's a smile which you took for a sneer;

One half of him contradicts t'other, his wont

Is to say very sharp things and do very blunt;

His manner 's as hard as his feelings are tender,

And a *sortie* he'll make when he means to surrender;

He's in joke half the time when he seems to be sternest,

When he seems to be joking, be sure he's in earnest;

He has common sense in a way that's uncommon,

Hates humbug and cant, loves his friends like a woman,

Builds his dislikes of cards and his friendships of oak,

Loves a prejudice better than aught but a joke,

Is half upright Quaker, half downright come-outer,

Loves Freedom too well to go stark mad about her,

Quite artless himself is a lover of art,

Shuts you out of his secrets and into his heart,

And though not a poet, yet all must admire

In his letters of Pinto his skill on the liar.

"There comes Poe with his raven-like Barnaby Rudge,

Three-fifths of him genius and two-fifths sheer fudge,

[margin annotations: "of the", "they", "it", "at least to my fancy"]

"A FABLE FOR CRITICS" PROOF-SHEET WITH LOWELL'S CORRECTIONS

From the original, kindly lent by Mrs. Charles F. Briggs, Brooklyn, N. Y.

In the period between the middle of 1847 and the end of 1849 he wrote most of the "Biglow Papers" of that series, he continued his regular work for the "Standard," and wrote the "Fable for Critics" and the "Vision of Sir Launfal." Mr. Lawrence Lowell says that the last was written in forty-eight hours, during which he scarcely slept or ate; and he considers it the most generally popular of the poet's longer poems.

Success gave him new stimulus, and in a happy home he worked with all the help which love and true sympathy could give him. To enter into the spirit of that life, one must make real what Mr. Lawrence Lowell has so well expressed. "He was, no doubt, to some extent a martyr for his political opinions, but no martyr was ever so high-spirited, so jovial, and so charming. As he said himself, he was curiously compounded of two utterly distinct characters. One half was clear mystic and enthusiast, the other humorist; and the humor, which is the best balance-wheel vouchsafed to man, prevented his remaining narrow or fanatical."

"On July 1, 1851, he embarked on a sailing vessel for Genoa, and passed most of the following year in Italy. A great part of the year was spent in Rome, with his lifelong friend, William Wetmore Story." But the charm of the earlier years was broken. His little Rose died in 1850; Walter, his only son, died two years later; Mrs. Lowell's health, always delicate, gave way, and she died in 1853, on the 27th of October, after they had returned to America.

His duty as professor at Cambridge began in September, 1856. Of some details in his discharge of this I have spoken in another chapter. He would refer, sometimes, to a certain "numbness" in literary effort which came from the monotony of a teacher's duties. But, as Mr. Lawrence Lowell says, when we remember that most of his prose books were written in the twenty years of his professorship, that in the same time he wrote "The Cathedral," the second series of the "Biglow Papers," the great "Commemoration Ode," and several of his best shorter poems, we feel that we must not take too seriously what he said of the numbing effect of the class-room.

Of "The Cathedral," after nearly thirty years, I may perhaps mention a contemporary criticism. When it was published, I was the editor of "Old and New." My theory was, and is, that generally a book should be reviewed by some one in sympathy with the author. So I sent "The Cathedral" to Mr. Waldo Emerson, hoping that he would write a review of it for our magazine. He returned the book the next day, saying that he could not write the article. When I met him next, I expressed my regret; and the philosopher said simply, "But, I *like* Lowell, I like Lowell." To which I replied, "Yes, and you like the poem, do you not?" "I like it — yes; but I think he had to pump." The figure is best understood by those of us who know the difference between "striking oil" and digging an artesian well for it and putting in valves and pistons with a steam-engine. Probably Lowell

WILLIAM WETMORE STORY

would have enjoyed the criticism as much as any one.

Lowell's own inside view of editing, and of the " Atlantic," the early career of which he directed, peeps out again and again in his letters.   If it were well to print here some of his private notes to contributors, they would, as I have intimated, show an almost motherly care of the new-born magazine. The first number is dated December, 1857, and in that month he writes, " Even the Magazine has its compensations."   Let the reader remember that the new duty he has undertaken, the " avocation," is superimposed on his " vocation," — the regular work of a full college professor.   " First, it has almost got me out of debt, and, next, it compels me into morning walks to the printing-office.   [This was the Riverside Press, not far from the college.] There is a little foot-path which leads along the river-bank, and it is lovely, whether in clear, cold mornings, when the fine filaments of the bare trees on the horizon seem floating up like sea-mosses in the ether sea, or when (as yesterday) a gray mist fills our Cambridge cup, and gives a doubtful loom to its snowy brim of hills, while the silent gulls wheel over the nestling cakes of ice which the Charles is whirling seaward."

If other editors had a morning walk like this, and had the eyes to see and the ears to hear, it might be well for other readers.

When one remembers that the Autocrat's papers were going on in the " Atlantic " at this time, that Motley and Prescott were publishing bits of their histories in it, that Longfellow wrote almost regularly in these numbers, and that younger writers, now well known, were winning their spurs in these first two volumes, it is easy to see that the work of the editor, who was easily chief among them, was interesting and inspiring to him. People were not then used to such papers as his on Choate and Cushing. He writes this scrap in October, 1858 : —

"Phillips was so persuaded of the stand given to the Magazine by the Choate article that he has been at me ever since for another. So I have been writing a still longer one on Cushing. I think you will like it, — though on looking over the Choate article I am inclined to think that, on the whole, the better of the two.

"The worst [of editing] is that it leads me to bore my friends when I do get at them. To be an editor is almost as bad as being President."

To Mr. Higginson, then forty years younger than he is now, he says, " As for your own contributions, I may say to you, as I always have to Mr. Underwood, that they are just to my liking, — scholarly, picturesque, and, above all, earnest, — I think the most *telling* essays we have printed."

And when he resigns the charge to his friend Fields — his warm friend till death — in May, 1861: "I was going to say I was glad to be rid of my old man of the sea. But I don't believe I am. A bore that is periodical gets a friendly face at last, and we miss it on the whole. . . .

" Well, good-by — delusive royalty ! I abdicate

with what grace I may.   I lay aside my paper crown and feather sceptre."

And in the same note he says he shall always gladly do what he can for the " Atlantic," a promise which he well fulfilled.   The second series of the " Biglow Papers " was published there.

In a way, perhaps, he had a right to feel that he, earlier than any one else, had the credit for the first fortunes of the " Atlantic," and to be proud of them.   To become the editor of the aged " North American," hand in hand with his near friend Mr. Norton, was a wholly different thing.

I am sure that there is somewhere, among his by-letters, an outburst as to what he will do " if he shall ever edit the ' North American.' "   I think most youngsters of his time — who were born with a pen in hand — indulged in the same dream, if they were bred within sound of the college bell at Cambridge.

In those prehistoric days the " North American," to the notions of the few hundred people who had ever heard of it, was wholly different from what any journal is now to any reader.   Four times a year only — quarterly ! — think of that, young contributors to to-day's " Atlantic " who can hardly live three weeks, to know if that horrid man has refused your poem, or if that charming and sensible editor has printed it !   Read Mrs. Lyman's Life, or any other good sketch of New England life in the twenties of this century, and see how people wrote or spoke of the arrival of the new " North American," with the

interest with which the inhabitants of Saturn might
speak of the regular decennial fall of some well-
timed aerolite!

The " North American " is now so different from
what it was in 1864, when Lowell took charge of it
with Mr. Norton, that its accomplished editor will
pardon me if I say ten words more about its infant
issues, to the young writers of this generation. It
was founded — modestly, yes, but with determination — among a little confident circle of the well-
trained young men of Boston, at a moment when
Boston counted, perhaps, fifty thousand people.
These were people who had time to read, and time
to write, and thought themselves, strange to say,
the rivals and equals of anybody in the world.
The quarterly was the then regnant fashion. The
Edinburgh " Quarterly," the London " Quarterly,"
were the arrogant dictators of English literature.
" Go to, now! We will dictate also! We will
have a 'Quarterly' of our own!" For one, I like
what the vernacular calls the " dander" of that
determination.

And some plucky and loyal bits of good American sentiment and statement got themselves into the
juvenile " North American." But it was awfully
proper. Its editors were more anxious about making
their " Quarterly " respectable in the eyes of their
ten English readers than of the thousand American
readers, more or less, who paid them five dollars a
year for their editing.

Now the remainder of the people of England and
of the people of America did not know that any

O.W.Holmes phot.
1864.

J.R. Lowell. Elmwood.

such "Quarterly" existed.   There had never risen
for it any publisher who "knew the American
people."

In one of the changes of literary "property," the
dwindling "list" of the now venerable Review fell
into the hands of people who had courage to give
Norton and Lowell the charge of it.   Soon after,
Fields, Osgood & Co. bought the Review.

"Norton and I have undertaken to edit the
'North American,'" Lowell writes.   "A rather
Sisyphean job, you will say.   It wanted three chief
elements to be successful.   It was n't thoroughly,
that is, thick and thinly, loyal; it was n't lively;
and it had no particular opinions on any particular subject.   It was an eminently safe periodical,
and accordingly was in great danger of running
aground."

To this "eminently safe" journal Mr. Norton and
Lowell undertook to give loyalty and life.   To the
little circle which followed in the steps, now falter-
ing, of the Mutual Admiration Club, they added
contributors from all latitudes and longitudes.
Thus the new departure is marked by letters asking
for articles, — to Motley in Vienna, Howells in
Venice, Stedman, who was a new writer for them;
and, as the reader has seen, Lowell's own work was
in amount what one would hardly have wished for
had the Review furnished his only occupation.

CHAPTER XI

In 1856, the year when Lowell's name first appears as a professor in the Harvard catalogue, he is one of eleven professors. In 1891, the year of his death, there were fifty-seven professors and assistant professors. The number of "tutors" and "instructors," to follow the college titles, increases in the same proportion. Lowell's name does not appear on the list of the "Faculty" in 1855, I suppose because he was in Europe. The Faculty consisted of thirteen gentlemen, of whom President Eliot, then one of the junior members, and Professor James Mills Peirce are now the only survivors. Of his associates in the Faculty, Dr. Walker and Professors Felton, Peirce, Bowen, and Lovering had been his teachers when he was himself an undergraduate twenty years before. Of the others, Professor Sophocles, older than he, had been Greek professor in Amherst before Lowell was at Cambridge. Professors Child, Lane, Jennison, Cooke, Chase, Eliot, and James Peirce were his juniors. In the cordial and simple courtesies of Cambridge life, all these gentlemen are to be spoken of in any calendar of his friends. After his college work begins, his name appears on the list of the Faculty. And it remains on the catalogue during the eight years when he was in Spain and England as American minister. He went to Europe in 1855, after his appointment as professor, and remained there more than a year; he made another visit in August, 1872, and remained abroad until July, 1874. His proper duties at Cambridge, therefore, were between September, 1856, and the summer of 1872, and from October, 1874, to his appointment as minister to Spain in the spring of 1877, covering in both periods nearly nineteen years.

The earlier of these periods — that from 1856 to 1872 — includes the whole civil war and the most acute of the struggles which preceded it. He watched with great interest the Kansas trials, and had at one time the idea of taking Hosea Biglow out to Kansas to send his prophecies from what was really the seat of war. He was himself learning, and the world was learning, that Minerva was not unwilling when he wrote prose; although it was as late as 1846 that he expressed himself so doubtfully in that matter. It is a pity that the best of his political essays, in the " Standard," in the " Atlantic," and in the " North American," cannot be published together. In the " Atlantic " and the " North American " there are, for instance, such articles as " The New Tariff Bill," " July reviewed by September," " The Election in November," " The Pickens-and-Stealin's-Rebellion," " The Question of the Hour," " The President's Policy," " The Rebellion, its Causes and Consequences," " Reconstruction," " Scotch the Snake or kill it?"

His cousin, Mr. Lawrence Lowell, thus character-
izes these essays : —

" During the period of war and reconstruction
Lowell wrote a number of political essays, but these
are not as remarkable as his poetry or his criticism.
Although very influential in forming public opinion,
and although containing many wise sayings and
many striking aphorisms on government, they are,
in the main, a forcible exposition of the opinions
held by intelligent Republicans. Beginning with a
distrust of Lincoln's tentative policy, they finally
express unbounded admiration for the statesmanship
that could wait until the times were ripe, and give
the lead when the people were ready to follow. The
essays show how thoroughly the writer had become
estranged from the abolitionists. He regards the
conflict at the outset, not as a crusade against slavery, but as a struggle to restore order and maintain the unity of the nation as a question of national existence, in which the peculiar institution of
the South is not at issue ; and, although before the
war was over he saw that no lasting peace was
possible unless slavery was forever destroyed, he
held that opinion in common with men who had
never harbored a thought of abolition before the
secession of South Carolina. In short, he no longer
writes as the prophet of 1848, but as a citizen and
a statesman."

In an earlier chapter I have already referred to
the " Anti-Slavery Standard," so long a brilliant
exception to the dullness, almost proverbial, of what
are called the " organs " of causes or of societies.

Lowell's connection with the "Standard" for many years brought him into close connection with a man after his own heart, Sydney Howard Gay, well known among all journalists, historians, and men of letters in America. He will be remembered for the untold services which he rendered to the country in and after the civil war, and to good letters, good history, and good journalism before the war, in the war, after the war, and, indeed, as long as he lived.

In 1840 it would have been difficult, even for a person inside the sacred circle of the abolitionists, to explain, in a manner satisfactory to every one, the difference between "old organization," "new organization," and the shades of feeling and thought in either, or among "come-outers" or "come-outer" societies, which were neither of the new nor old. For an outsider it would have been impossible to make such explanations then. And, fortunately, any such discrimination is now as unnecessary as it is impossible. They were all free lances, who obeyed any leader when they chose, and, if they did not like his direction, told him so and refused to follow. A sufficient section of anti-slavery people, however, to carry out their purposes, established the "Anti-Slavery Standard."

At a meeting quite celebrated in those times, in which the original Anti-Slavery Society divided itself between what was called the "old organization" and the "new organization," the old organization, sometimes called the "Garrisonians," determined to establish this paper. This was in the year 1840, and the first editor was a gentleman named

Nathaniel P. Rogers, a brilliant and vigorous writer from New Hampshire. He died in 1846. His essays have been published, with a Life by John Pierpont.

The motto of the new journal was " Without concealment and without compromise." It was under the general superintendence of what is spoken of afterwards as the " executive committee ; " and, if I understand it rightly, this executive committee was chosen annually at the meetings of the " old organization." An outsider, perhaps, would have said that Garrison's " Liberator " would answer the purpose of an organ ; and, so far as devotion to the main cause went, of course it would. But Garrison, on his part, would never have ground the crank of anybody's organ. And, on the other side, the Anti-Slavery Society did not want, as such, to accompany him on such side-crusades as he might wish to undertake in the course of the great enterprise. For an instance, most, if not all, of the people who united to establish the " Standard " would choose to vote, if they wanted to do so, and frequently did vote. But he whom in those days men called an abolitionist pure and simple, whom one could underwrite as A 1, would have abominated any vote at any election.

This was the explanation given me by the person best qualified to answer my question when I asked, " Why the ' National Anti-Slavery Standard ' *and* the ' Liberator ' ? "

In 1844 Mr. Gay became the editor of the " Standard." He was an abolitionist through and through.

He even gave up the study of law, because he felt that he could not swear to sustain the Constitution of the United States, and so could not enter at the bar. He had very rare gifts of editorial promptness and sagacity ; and, as the " Standard " itself shows, had the unselfishness and the knowledge of men which enabled him to engage as fellow-workmen men and women of remarkable ability. Henry Wilson speaks of him as the man who deserved well of his country because he kept the " Tribune " a war paper in spite of Greeley.

Lowell had written before 1846 for the anti-slavery papers, as the reader knows. Mrs. Chapman, a lady distinguished among the abolitionists, had suggested to Gay that Lowell would give strength to the " Standard." How droll it seems now that anybody should be advising anybody to engage his services ! All the same, Mrs. Chapman did, and he was retained to write once a week for the "Standard." In an early letter of his to Gay, as early as June of 1846, he says that he is " totally unfitted " for the position of an " editorial contributor." He was sure that Garrison and Mrs. Chapman overrated his popularity. " In the next place," — this is edifying now, — " if I have any vocation, it is the making of verse. When I take my pen for that, the world opens itself ungrudgingly before me, everything seems clear and easy, as it seems sinking to the bottom would be as one leans over the edge of his boat in one of those dear coves at Fresh Pond. But when I do prose, it is *invitâ Minervâ*. My true place is to serve the cause as a poet."

In the same letter he suggests what we now call a " funny column." He calls it a " Weekly Pasquil." " I am sure I come across enough comical thoughts in a week to make up a good share of such a corner, and Briggs and yourself [Gay] and Quincy could help."

Edmund Quincy began in the " Standard " that series of letters signed " Byles," which with infinite fun and spirit revealed Boston to the decorous senses of those people who had supposed that they were the " upper four hundred." The letters were afterward carried on in the " Tribune " for many years. In this instance, as in the transfer of Mr. Gay's services to the " Tribune," the " Standard " led the way for some of the signal achievements in the interesting history of that paper.

Lowell's correspondence with Gay is excellent reading for young men who have fallen in love with their own picture of journalism, and are fascinated by the charm of that picture. To us, reading after fifty years, it is edifying, not to say amusing, to find that, after rather more than a year, the " Executive Committee " of the " Standard " feared that they were flinging their money away in paying this young poet four dollars and eighty cents a week for his contributions. Think of that, gentlemen who manage the treasuries of weekly or monthly journals now! James Lowell, in the very prime of his life, is writing for you. He is just beginning on the " Biglow Papers." And you find that the work is not worth five dollars a week, and notify your working editor that he must be dropped!

Lowell's letter in reply is manly and courteous. He even says that he has felt somewhat cramped by the knowledge that a corresponding editor ought to recognize the views of an "Executive Committee." "I have felt that I ought to work in my own way, and yet I have also felt that I ought to try to work in their way, so that I have failed of working in either."

Young authors may read with interest these words, — not too proud: "I think the Executive Committee would have found it hard to get some two or three of the poems I have furnished from any other quarter." "Beaver Brook," for instance, "To Lamartine," or several of the early Biglow papers! No! It would be hard to get them furnished "from any other quarter." And the anonymous Executive Committee flinched at the four dollars and eighty cents which had to be paid for each of these! With one and another such jar, however, the connection between Lowell and the "Standard" lasted, in one or another form, for four or five years.

I hope it is not too late for us still to expect a full memoir of Mr. Gay's life and work. As a permanent contribution to literature, "The Popular History of America" will preserve his memory. It is the first of the composite histories wrought by the hands of many experts; but it all went under his careful supervision, and ought to be called by his name. At Chicago, at New York, in the "Tribune," and as coadjutor with Mr. Bryant in the "Evening Post" office, he showed what his great capacity as an editor was.

I have never seen in print his story of that fearful night when Lincoln was killed. But one hears it freely repeated in conversation, and I see no reason why it should not be printed now.

With the news of the murder of Lincoln, there came to New York every other terrible message. The office of the "Tribune," of course, received echoes from all the dispatches which showed the alarm at Washington. There were orders for the arrest of this man, there were suspicions of the loyalty of that man. No one knew what the morrow might bring.

In the midst of the anxieties of such hours, to Mr. Gay, the acting editor of that paper, there entered the foreman of the typesetting-room. He brought with him the proof of Mr. Greeley's leading article, as he had left it before leaving the city for the day. It was a brutal, bitter, sarcastic, personal attack on President Lincoln, — the man who, when Gay read the article, was dying in Washington.

Gay read the article, and asked the foreman if he had any private place where he could lock up the type, to which no one but himself had access. The foreman said he had. Gay bade him tie up the type, lock the galley with this article in his cupboard, and tell no one what he had told him. Of course no such article appeared in the "Tribune" the next morning.

But when Gay arrived on the next day at the office, he was met with the news that "the old man" wanted him, and the intimation that "the old man" was very angry. Gay waited upon Greeley.

SYDNEY HOWARD GAY

"Are you there, Mr. Gay? I have been looking for you. They tell me that you ordered my leader out of this morning's paper. Is it your paper or mine? I should like to know if I cannot print what I choose in my own newspaper!" This in great rage.

"The paper is yours, Mr. Greeley. The article is in type upstairs, and you can use it when you choose. Only this, Mr. Greeley: I know New York, and I hope and believe, before God, that there is so much virtue in New York that, if I had let that article go into this morning's paper, there would not be one brick upon another in the 'Tribune' office now. Certainly I should be sorry if there were."

Mr. Greeley was cowed. He said not a word, nor ever alluded to the subject again. I suppose the type is locked up in the cupboard of the "Tribune" office at this hour.

It was by this sort of service that Mr. Gay earned Mr. Wilson's praise that "he kept Mr. Greeley up to the war."

Mr. Lowell's correspondence with Mr. Gay makes one wish that we had Mr. Gay's side as well. The letters which are printed in Lowell's "Correspondence" are well worthy the study of young journalists.

It will be readily seen that here was a college professor well in touch with the responsibilities of the time. Writing occasionally for such a paper as the "Standard," responsible for the tone and politics of the "Atlantic," and afterwards of the "North American," he could tell the world what he thought

in those times of storm and earthquake; and he did
not fail to use his opportunity.   Meanwhile the war
was drawing nearer and nearer.   Strictly speaking,
the war began when Franklin Pierce, on the part
of the government of the United States, acting by
the United States marshal, took possession of the
Hotel of the Emigrant Aid Company, in Lawrence,
Kansas, in May, 1856, and destroyed it.

The class of youngsters who entered Harvard
College in 1856, when Lowell began his work there,
graduated in 1860, and were eager to go into the
army.   Of that class sixty-four enlisted, of whom
thirteen were killed.   Thirty-six of the next class
enlisted in the army or navy; thirty of the next
class; and thirty-two of the class of 1863.   Lowell
was in personal relations with most of these young
men.   He had five young relatives who died in the
service, — General Charles Russell Lowell and his
brother James Jackson Lowell, William Lowell Putnam, Warren Dutton Russell, and Francis Lowell
Dutton Russell, who was only twenty when he died.
William Putnam was the son of the sister whose
account of the childhood of Lowell has been already
referred to.

Mr. Leslie Stephen has referred pathetically to
Lowell's white-heat patriotism as the war went on,
— he watching it with such associations.   " The
language of the most widely known English newspapers at the time could hardly have been more
skillfully framed for the purpose of irritating Lowell,
if it had been consciously designed to that end. . . .
He showed me the photograph of a young man in

the uniform of the United States army, and asked
me whether I thought that that lad looked like 'a
blackguard.' On my giving the obvious reply, he
told me that the portrait represented one of the
nephews he had lost in the war. Not long afterward I read his verses in the second series of the
'Biglow Papers,' the most pathetic, I think, that he
ever wrote, in which he speaks of the 'three likely
lads,'

> 'Whose comin' step there's ears thet won't,
> No, not lifelong, leave off awaitin'.' "

These "three likely lads" were General Charles
Russell Lowell, his brother James Jackson Lowell,
and William Lowell Putnam, their cousin and the
poet's nephew.

In the autumn of 1860 Charles Lowell took charge
of the Mount Savage Iron Works at Cumberland,
Maryland. On the 20th of April, 1861, hearing of
the attack made the preceding day in Baltimore on
the Sixth Massachusetts Regiment, Lowell instantly
abandoned his position and set out for Washington.
He put himself at once at the disposal of the government, and about the middle of June received his
commission as captain in the Third Regiment of
United States Cavalry. For distinguished services
at Williamsburg and Slatersville he was nominated
for the brevet of Major. At South Mountain, in
bearing orders to General Reno, he showed a bravery
which excited universal admiration. In recognition
of his gallantry in this battle, General McClellan
assigned to Lowell the duty of presenting to the
President the trophies of the campaign. In Novem-

ber, 1862, he was ordered to report to Governor
Andrew for the purpose of organizing the Second
Massachusetts Cavalry, of which he was appointed
Colonel. In the May following he left Boston with
his regiment, and was soon placed in command
of the cavalry of the Department of Washington.
For many months he was occupied in resisting the
incursions of Mosby. "I have often said," writes
Colonel Mosby, "that of all the Federal commanders
opposed to me, I had the highest respect for Colonel
Lowell, both as an officer and as a gentleman." It
was at Cedar Creek, while leading his command,
that he received his mortal wound. His commission
as Brigadier-General of Volunteers, "determined on
days before," was signed on the 19th of October,
too late for him to wear the honor he had earned so
well. "We all shed tears," said Custer, "when we
knew we had lost him."

General Lowell's brother, James Jackson Lowell,
was but twenty-three years old when the war began.
He was born in the very Elmwood where, as this
writer hopes, this reader feels at home. His early
youth was spent in Boston, where he was a student
in the Public Latin School. Before he entered college, the family had removed to Cambridge again.

He spent the four years from 1854 as an undergraduate in Cambridge, taking his bachelor's degree
in 1858, at the second Commencement after his
uncle entered on his duties there. He took the
highest place in his class when he graduated; a
favorite with his class, "liked as much as he was
admired." "While he would walk a dozen miles

ELMWOOD

From a photograph by Miss C. E. Peabody, Cambridge, Mass.

for wild flowers, skate all day, and dance as long as
the music would play, he found no study too dry,
and would have liked to embrace all science and all
literature."

He showed the interest in public affairs which
such a young man ought to show, and such as was
suggested to him by his ancestry on his father's
side and his mother's alike. He was at the Dane
Law School, — the school connected with the University at Cambridge, — when the war broke out.
James Lowell and his cousin, William Putnam, also
at the Law School, undertook to raise recruits for
a Massachusetts regiment. After some delay they
and their recruits were assigned to the Twentieth
Regiment, Lowell taking a commission as First
Lieutenant, and Putnam that of Second. They
received their commissions on the 10th of July.
They were sent to the front in September.

After a few days in Washington they were
ordered to Poolesville in Maryland, and they were
encamped there until October 20. On the 21st of
October they were led across the Potomac by General Lane, who atoned for this mistake by his life.
The wretched and useless battle of Ball's Bluff
was fought, Putnam was so severely wounded that
he died in a few days, Schmitt, their captain, was
wounded, and Lowell shot in his thigh. He returned home until his wound was healed, and joined
his regiment on the Potomac as the movement of
McClellan against Richmond went forward. He saw
rather than joined in the fighting at Fair Oaks, and
on the 26th of June writes, in good spirits, that

he has hopes of seeing Richmond before the month is over. But, alas! on the 29th the regiment was ordered to join McClellan's retreat to the Potomac, and on the 30th he received a mortal wound at Glendale.

His cousin, William Lowell Putnam, was an only son. The friend and teacher of the two, Professor Child, says: "A nobler pair never took the field. Putnam, with his fair hair, deep eyes, and uncontaminated countenance, was the impersonation of knightly youth. He was our Euryalus, *quo pulchrior alter non fuit Æneadum.* The cousins were beautifully matched in person, mental accomplishments, and pure heroism of character."

I copy Professor Child's words with a certain special tenderness for a personal remembrance of "Willie Putnam," as most of his friends called him. I was in Salignac's drill corps, before the war began, at a time when the drill was carried on in a large hall, at the corner of Summer Street and Washington Street in Boston. The hall was not long enough for the battalion to form in line, and two right angles were necessary, so that we stood at parade with our backs to three sides of the wall. Day by day, for I know not how many weeks, in presenting arms at parade, I "presented arms," not so much to the commanding officer, as to this beautiful boy, who at the distance of thirty or forty yards presented arms to me. Among three or four hundred young men, most of them younger than I, I did not know his name. In June he was enlisting men, and Salignac and the drill corps, and I

ROBERT GOULD SHAW

WILLIAM LOWELL PUTNAM   CHARLES RUSSELL LOWELL

JAMES JACKSON LOWELL

among the rest, saw him no longer. In October
he was killed ; and then for the first time, when I
saw his picture, did I know that the noble, cheerful
face I had so often saluted was that of this fine
young man, in whose career, for many reasons, I
was interested so deeply.

Such were three of five relatives who went to the
war, almost from Elmwood itself. One sees how
Lowell's personal interest in them affected all he
wrote in poetry or prose in the great crisis.

Professor Child, whom I cited in the passage
above, took the most eager interest in the war, as,
indeed, in one way or another, all the professors at
Cambridge did. He was one of the Faculty who
had joined it since they dragged Lowell through
college " by the hair of his head," as he and Cutler
dragged Loring through. Eager in everything in
the way of public spirit, Professor Child made it his
special duty to prepare a " Song-book " for the sol-
diers who were going to the field. Who is doing it
now for the liberators of to-day ? He made everybody who could, write a war-song, and he printed a
little book of these songs, with the music, which
he used to send to the front with every marching
regiment. I had the pleasure of telling him once
that I had heard one of his songs sung by some privates of our Twenty-fourth in the camp before Ber-
muda Hundred. This curious collection is already
rare. It was called " War Songs for Freemen," and
was dedicated to the army of the United States.
Professor Child enlisted Charles T. Brooks, the
Newport poet, Dr. Hedge, Dr. Holmes, and Mrs.

Howe, both the Lelands, Mrs. T. Sedgwick, and
some anonymous writers, to join in furnishing songs.
He included some good translations from the German.   He wrote two or three himself, which show
his fun and audacity.   Here is the last verse of
" The Lass of the Pamunky : " —

> " Fair hands ! but not too nice or coy
>   To soothe my pangs with service tender.
> Soft eyes ! that watched a wasted boy,
>   All loving, as your land's defender ! —
> Oh ! I was then a wretched shade,
>   But now I 'm strong and growing chunky —
> So Forward ! and God bless the maid
>   That saved my life on the Pamunky ! "

Here is a new verse of " Lilliburlero : "—

> " ' Well, Uncle Sam,' says Jefferson D.,
>   Lilliburlero, Old Uncle Sam,
> ' You 'll have to join my Confed'racy,'
>   Lilliburlero, Old Uncle Sam.
> ' Lero, lero, that don't appear, O ! That don't appear,' says Old
>   Uncle Sam.
> ' Lero, lero, filibustero ! That don't appear,' says Old Uncle Sam."

Mr. Child was appointed professor in rhetoric in
1851, and by a new appointment in 1876 professor
of the English language and literature.   It is interesting to see that, although the use of the English
language had been admirably taught at Harvard
long before, there was no professor of English literature for two centuries and a half after the college
was founded.   Is there one at Oxford or at the
English Cambridge to-day ?

How well fitted Mr. Child was for these positions
his published series of ballads and other works show.
His recent death gives me a right to speak here of

FRANCIS JAMES CHILD

the tender love with which he was regarded by all
the Cambridge circle, and of the unselfish interest
with which he gave time and work to the help of
all around him. One is glad to see this interest
surviving in the lives of his children.

I am not sure that this story of those days is
quite decorous enough for print. But I will risk it.
Professor Calvin Ellis Stowe, who was a classmate
of Longfellow's, told me that in the early days
of '61 he met Longfellow in the streets of Boston.
Both of them were in haste, but Longfellow had
time enough to ask if the Andover gentlemen were
all alive to their duty to the nation. Stowe said
he thought they were, and Longfellow said, " If the
New Testament won't do, you must give them the
Old." Professor Stowe told me this in August of
1861, after the anniversary exercises of the class
at Andover. The division between Rehoboam and
Jeroboam had naturally played a very important
part in the chapel exercises, with the obvious distinction that in our time it was the North which was
in the right and the South which was in the wrong.

I am permitted to copy the following scraps from
the journal of one of Lowell's pupils at that time : —

" In '64, when I had come back from a service
mostly civil, but under direction of General Saxton,
on Port Royal Islands, I had to give the college
steward a bond to secure whatever dues I might
incur. Lowell volunteered to sign the bond, and to
say that he had perfect confidence in me. December 22 he called at Divinity Hall, to invite me to
a five o'clock Christmas dinner ; again on Christmas

to turn the hour into four o'clock. The other
guests were John Holmes and Caroline Norton, a
young man and a niece of the host. Each man
was impressed into escort duty to a woman, and
I was Mabel's escort to the table.

"The dinner and the chat were delightful.
Holmes and Lowell sharpened their wits upon each
other, while the rest of us ate and laughed. I was
the only obdurate that would not take a smile of
wine. After dinner we were entertained with some
of Blake's curious pictures, with snowflake shapes,
and with books. Lowell had been 'weeding his
back garden,' and he offered me the little stock of
duplicates and obsoletes: a Webster's quarto dictionary was one of the books, and the evening was
Christmas; but the boys had a notion that his income was almost pinchingly small for a man in his
place; so, in the hope that he might second-hand
them off for five or ten dollars, I declined them,
and have been sorry ever since. I should have
known that if he wanted to sell them he would not
even have shown them to me, and that he did want
to put them where they would be helpful and well
used."

I might almost say that such daily associations
with the war account for the form and spirit alike
of the "Commemoration Ode." No one who was
present when that ode was delivered can forget the
occasion. It was in every regard historical. Peace
was concluded, and the country drew a long breath
with joy for the first time. An immense assembly
of the graduates came together. As many of them

HENRY WADSWORTH LONGFELLOW (1860)

as could filed into the church for religious services.
Under the lead of Mr. Paine, the professor of music,
a college chorus sang "Salvam fac rempublicam."
I think this was the first time that the music now
well known was used for those words.   On such
occasions at Cambridge the graduates entered the
church in the order of their seniority.   I remember
that on that occasion the attendance was so large
that my own class, which was twenty-six years out
of college, were among the last persons who could
enter the building.   We stood in the aisles, because
there were no seats for us.

After these services the whole body of the alumni
sat at a Spartan college feast in that part of " the
yard," as we say at Cambridge, which is between
Harvard and Holden Halls.   And there Lowell delivered his "Commemoration Ode."   His own intense
interest was evident enough, but it was reflected in
what I might call the passionate interest with which
people heard.   It was said afterwards, and I think
this appears in his letters, that the final business of
writing this wonderful poem had all been done in
forty-eight hours before he delivered it.   But then,
as the reader sees, it had been more than four years
in the writing.   The inspiration had come from day
to day, and he poured out here the expression of
what he had been thinking and feeling, in joy and
sorrow, in hope and fear, in learning and forgetting, for all that period of crisis and strain.

I believe I may tell — and it shall close these
broken reminiscences of the war — a story which
was familiarly told at the time, and which is true.

I have heard it in one or two forms, and to secure accuracy now I have asked the gentleman whom I may call the hero of the story for his own account of it. He was one of Lowell's pupils, in the "battle class" of 1862. He has sent it to me in the following words : —

"I spent the night before Commemoration Day on a lounge in Hollis 21, the room of my classmate Hudson, who was a tutor. I could not afterwards remember dreaming of anything in particular ; but as I woke I *heard*,

> 'And what they dare to dream of, dare to die for.'

"'Rather a good sentiment,' I said to myself ; 'and it seems to be appropriate to the day,' — then just dawning. And so I dropped off again.

"The dinner was spread, as you remember, in the green bounded by Harvard, Hollis, and Holden. My seat was just about in the middle. Mr. Lowell was a few rods nearer Holden and a good deal nearer Hollis, — about under the more southerly window of Hollis 21. When he rose, there was a prolonged closing of the ranks, — I remember the rustle of many feet on the grass, — and Mr. Lowell waited till all was quiet before he began reading. As he read, when he came to the words,

> 'Their higher instinct knew
> Those love her best,' —

I began to feel, not that I had heard this before, but that *something familiar was coming*.

> 'Who to themselves are true,'

went on the reader. 'Hullo !' said I to myself, 'I ought to know the next line.'

'And what they dare' —

"'Yes, but it is n't going to rhyme,' and this without distinctly repeating the rest of the line."

When my friend had observed that "die for" would not rhyme with "true," Lowell came to his relief by saying,

"And what they dare to dream of, dare to do."

So well authenticated a story of sympathy and telepathy seems worth repeating.

CHAPTER XII

MR. LOWELL's real connection with the daily work of the college ceased in 1876, when he accepted the offer of the mission to Spain. It covered the period when he wrote most, and when, as his cousin has said so well, in the passage I have cited, his work in prose and poetry proved to be most satisfactory to himself. His duty afterwards as a diplomatist, in Spain and in England, was of value to the country and of credit to himself. And his life as a man of letters had prepared him for such work. But, all the same, it is as a man of letters that he will be most generally remembered.

During the twenty-one years from 1855 to 1876 the college was going through the change which has made it the university which it is. It had not only enlarged in the number of pupils, but the purposes and range of all persons connected with it widened with every year. This change from the "seminary," as President Quincy used to call it, to the university of to-day has not been wrought by any spasmodic revolution planned by either of the governing bodies at any given time. It has come about, healthy and strong, in the growth of the country — let us even say in the improvement of the world.

Presidents Quincy, Everett, Sparks, and Walker were all engaged in promoting the evolution of the university. After the close of that series come Thomas Hill and Charles William Eliot, the present incumbent, to whose energy, foresight, and courage so much of what may be called this revolution is due. I have already made some notes here of Mr. Quincy and Dr. Walker. It was in Walker's administration that Lowell returned to the college as Smith professor.

Cornelius Conway Felton, who succeeded Dr. Walker, had been the Greek professor, and had distinguished himself in his place as an editor of Homer and in papers on subjects of Greek literature. Perhaps he soon wore out his hopes for classes of schoolboys. Certainly in my time and Lowell's, when we were undergraduates, he made little or no effort as a teacher to open out the work of the Greek poets whom we read. Alkestis or the Iliad were literally mere text-books. All the same, the boys believed in Felton. I remember one scene of great excitement when he was a professor, when we thought we were very badly used by the government, as perhaps we were. There was a great crowd of us in front of Holworthy, and Felton appeared on the steps of Stoughton or at a window. Somebody shouted, "Hear Felton! hear Felton! he tells us the truth," and the noisy mob was still to listen. A man might be glad to have these words carved on his tombstone.

When with other men of letters, Dr. Felton was charming. And his kindness to his old pupils till they died was something marvelous. The published

Sumner letters, the Longfellow letters, and other correspondence of the men of that time, with many of his careful reviews, and an occasional pamphlet, perhaps on some subject of controversy now forgotten, show how highly he was prized in his day and how well he deserved such esteem. For many years he was one of the most acceptable writers for the "North American Review." He died, suddenly, after less than two years of service as President.

President Felton's successor, Thomas Hill, was a graduate of Harvard, as all her presidents have been since Chauncy died in 1672. Dr. Hill was of a noble family, — if we count nobility on the true standards, — who were driven out of England by the Birmingham riots of 1791, and settled near Philadelphia. Dr. Hill was appointed president of Antioch College, Ohio, in 1859, and, after a very successful administration there, he was inaugurated at Cambridge in 1862. At Antioch he had succeeded Horace Mann in the presidency.

Dr. Hill's health failed, and he resigned in 1868, leaving behind him charming memories of his devotion to duty and of the simplicity of his character. I called upon him once, with Dr. Newman Hall, when he was in this country. It was delightful to see the enthusiasm with which Dr. Hill spoke of the pleasure he expected in the evenings of the approaching winter, from studying, with his charming wife, the new text of the Syriac version of the New Testament, which had then just been edited by Cureton. He was one of the most distinguished mathematicians of his time. Here is an amusing note to him from Lowell about the arboriculture of the college yard.

My dear Dr. Hill, — I have been meaning to speak to you for some time about something which I believe you are interested in as well as myself, and, not having spoken, I make occasion to write this note. Something ought to be done about the trees in the college yard. That is my thesis, and my corollary is that you are the man to do it. They remind me always of a young author's first volume of poems. There are too many of 'em, and too many of one kind. If they were not planted in such formal rows, they would typify very well John Bull's notion of " our democracy," where every tree is its neighbor's enemy, and all turn out scrubs in the end, because none can develop fairly. Then there is scarce anything but American elms. I have nothing to say against the tree in itself. I have some myself whose trunks I look on as the most precious baggage I am responsible for in the journey of life ; but planted as they are in the yard, there 's no chance for one in ten. If our buildings so nobly dispute architectural preëminence with cotton mills, perhaps it is all right that the trees should become spindles ; but I think Hesiod (who knew something of country matters) was clearly right in his half being better than the whole, and nowhere more so than in the matter of trees. There are two English beeches in the yard which would become noble trees if the elms would let 'em alone. As it is, they are in danger of starving. Now, as you

are our Kubernetes, I want you to take the 'elm in
hand. We want more variety, more grouping. We
want to learn that one fine tree is worth more than
any mob of second-rate ones. We want to take
a leaf out of Chaucer's book, and understand that
in a stately grove every tree must " stand well from
his fellow apart." A doom hangs over us in the
matter of architecture, but if we will only let a tree
alone, it will build itself with a nobleness of proportion and grace of detail that Giotto himself might
have envied. Nor should the pruning as now be
trusted to men who get all they cut off, and whose
whole notion of pruning, accordingly, is " ax and
it shall be given unto you." Do, pray, take this
matter into your own hands — for you know how
to love a tree — and give us a modern instance of a
wise saw. Be remembered among your other good
things as the president that planted the groups of
evergreens for the wind to dream of the sea in all
summer, and for the snowflakes to roost on all
winter, and believe me (at the end of my sheet,
though not of my sermon) always cordially yours,

J. R. LOWELL.

ELMWOOD, December 8, 1863.

After President Hill's resignation, Dr. Andrew
Preston Peabody acted as president until the
appointment in 1869 of Mr. Eliot.

I have already spoken, in one connection or another, of the professors to whom Lowell was most
closely drawn, — with one or two exceptions. Dr.
Asa Gray, the distinguished chief of botany in

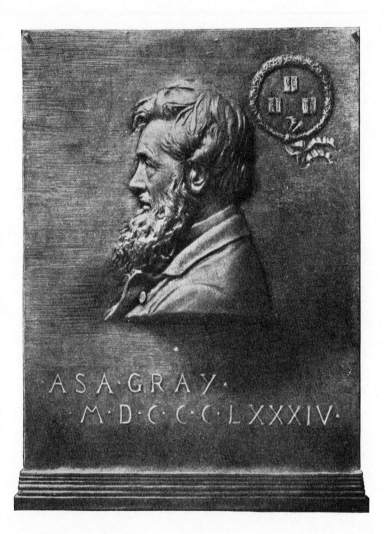

ASA·GRAY·
M·D·C·C·C·L·XXXIV·

America, made his home a centre of all that was charming and interesting in the delightful circle of Cambridge society. Nothing could be more interesting than the simplicity of the spirited conversation of this most learned man, and the ease with which, while he really knew almost everything that was worth knowing, he spoke, with utter absence of effect or visible erudition. Where a working gardener would tell you with delight that this or that plant was the " *Tomfoolaria eruditissima*," Gray would say, " Oh! that's one of those Australian sandworts." When he was still as fresh and cheerful as a boy, I heard him say, " It is great fun to be seventy years old. You do not have to know everything."

Another of his colleagues who gave distinction to the college, in America and in Europe, was the late Josiah Parsons Cooke, whose position as a teacher and in the ranks of original students in chemistry is so well known.

Lowell's own charming poem to Agassiz will be recalled by every one who cares for his life at Harvard. Not long after Agassiz had been invited from Switzerland to lecture before the Lowell Institute, he was appointed to a professorship in Cambridge, and he accepted the appointment. He lived in Cambridge from that time until he died, loving and beloved, in 1873. Mr. John Amory Lowell, the cousin of our Lowell, in his plans for the Lowell Institute, engaged Louis Agassiz to deliver one of their courses in 1847. His arrival in America may be spoken of as marking an era in education.

Indeed, if the Lowell Institute had never done anything else for America than it did when it " imported Agassiz," it would have a perpetual claim for our gratitude. With his arrival there was ended, once and forever, the poor habit of studying Nature through the eyes of other observers. Men learned again the lesson which makes them see where they look. For it may be fairly said that Agassiz created here the school of original study which has for a generation past directed the progress of natural science in America. I believe I ought to say that the phrase " imported Agassiz," which I have ventured to quote, is Lowell's own. In his address at the Quarter-Millennial of the college he had the hardihood to say that Harvard had not yet developed any first-rate educator, " for we imported Agassiz."

I have never forgotten the enthusiasm of Agassiz's audience the first time I ever heard him. His subject was the First Ascent of the Jungfrau, the maiden mountain which had never been scaled by man until Agassiz led the way. He told us, with eager memory, of all the preparations made for what men thought the hopeless invasion of those untrodden snows, of the personnel of the party, of their last night and early morning start at some encampment halfway up ; and then, almost step by step, of the sheer ascent at the last, until, man by man, one after another, each man stood alone, where two cannot stand together, on that little triangle of rock which is the summit. " And I looked down into Swisserland." As I heard him utter these simple words of

LOUIS AGASSIZ

triumph, I said that Mr. Lowell might take credit
to himself for bringing before our audience the noblest and best specimen, so far discovered, of that
greatest species of mammalia — long studied, but
as yet little known — of the very finest type, from
the widely scattered genus of the race of MAN.

The simplicity of Agassiz's mode of address cap-
tivated all hearers. He put himself at once in touch
with the common-school teachers. He had none of
that absurd conceit which has sometimes parted college professors from sympathetic work with their
brothers and sisters who have the first duty, in the
district and town schools, in the infinite work of
instruction and education.

Agassiz's Cambridge life brought into Cambridge
a good many of his European friends, and broke
up the strictness of a village coterie by the accent,
not to say the customs, of cosmopolitan life. To
say true, the denizens of the forest sometimes inter-
mixed closely with the well-trained European scholars.
There used to be a fine story of a dinner-party at
Dr. Arnold Guyot's when he lived at Cambridge.
An admiring friend had sent Guyot as a present
a black bear, which was confined in the cellar of
his house. Another friend had sent him a little
barrel of cider, which was also in the cellar. As the
dinner went on upstairs, ominous rumblings were
heard below, and suddenly an attendant rushed in
on the feast, announcing that the bear had got loose,
had been drinking the cider, had got drunk, and
was now coming upstairs. The guests fled through
windows and doors. I am not sure that Lowell was

one of them, but the anecdote belongs in notices of his friends.

I should not dare speak of a " village coterie," nor intimate that at Cambridge there were men who had never heard of Fujiyama, or of places, indeed, not twenty miles away, but that these anecdotes belong a generation and more ago.

One of Lowell's fellow professors told me this curious story, which will illustrate the narrowness of New England observation at that time. There appeared at Cambridge in the year 1860 a young gentleman named Robert Todd Lincoln, who has been already quoted, and is quite well known in this country and in England. This young man wished to enter Harvard College, and his father, one Abraham Lincoln, who has since been known in the larger world, had fortified him with a letter of introduction to Dr. Walker, the president of the college. This letter of introduction was given by one Stephen A. Douglas, who was a person also then quite well known in political life, and he presented the young man to Dr. Walker as being the son of his friend Abraham Lincoln, " with whom I have lately been canvassing the State of Illinois." When this letter, now so curious in history, was read, Lowell said to my friend who tells me the story, " I suppose I am the only man in this room who has ever heard of this Abraham Lincoln ; but he is the person with whom Douglas has been traveling up and down in Illinois, canvassing the State in their new Western fashion, as representatives of the two parties, each of them being the candidate for the vacant seat in the Senate." What is more, my friend says it is probably true that at the moment when this letter was presented by young Robert Lincoln, none of the faculty of Harvard College, excepting Lowell, had ever heard of Abraham Lincoln. The story is a good one, as showing how far it was in those days possible for a circle of intelligent men to know little or nothing of what was happening in the world beyond the sound of their college bell.[1]

It would be almost of course that, in a series of reminiscences which are not simply about Lowell but about his friends, I should include some careful history of the Saturday Club, which has held its regular meetings up to this time from the date of the dinner-party given by Mr. Phillips, as already described in the history of the "Atlantic." But that story has been so well told by Mr. Morse in his memoir of Dr. Holmes, and by Mr. Cooke in the "New England Magazine," that I need hardly do more than repeat what has been said before. In Morse's "Life of Dr. Holmes" there are two pages of admirably well-selected pictures of some of the members best known. When the reader sees the names of gentlemen who have attended the club more or less regularly in forty years, he will readily understand why Emerson and Holmes and Lowell and others of their contemporaries have spoken of the talk there as being as good talk as they had

[1] This anecdote arrested attention when it was first published, and I received more than one note explaining to me that it could not be true.

All the same it is true. And I took care to verify the dates of the several steps of the story.

ever heard anywhere. Holmes's list, besides himself, was Emerson, Hawthorne, Longfellow, Lowell, Motley, Whipple, Whittier, Professors Agassiz and Peirce; John Sullivan Dwight, Governor Andrew, Richard Henry Dana, Jr., and Charles Sumner, Presidents Felton and Eliot, Professors Norton and Goodwin, William Hickling Prescott, Thomas Gold Appleton, John Murray Forbes, John Elliot Cabot, Henry James, William Dean Howells, Thomas Bailey Aldrich, William Morris Hunt, Charles Francis Adams, Francis Parkman, James Freeman Clarke, Judge Lowell, Judge Hoar, George Frisbie Hoar, and Bishop Brooks.

One of the last times when I saw Lowell and Emerson together was on the 18th of July, 1867, when Emerson delivered his second Phi Beta Kappa address. It had never happened before, I think, that the same orator should have spoken twice before Phi Beta Kappa with an interval of thirty years between the orations; nor is it probable that such a thing will ever happen again. In 1837 the word Transcendentalist was new, and it was considered "good form" to ridicule the Transcendentalists, and especially to ridicule Emerson. Yet he had his admirers then, especially his admirers in college, where the recollections of his poetry and philosophy, as shown when he was an undergraduate, had not died out. A few years ago I printed his two Bowdoin prize dissertations, written when he was seventeen and eighteen years of age, and they are enough to show that the boy, at that age, was father of the man. When he spoke in 1837, the oration was

CHARLES ELIOT NORTON

received in a certain patronizing way by his seniors.
Mr. Cabot says, " He was regarded as a promising
young beginner, from whom a fair poetical speech
might be expected," and the address was spoken of
with a gay badinage such as could not be called
criticism. I remember, at the frugal dinner-party
of Phi Beta Kappa after the oration of 1837, Mr.
Edward Everett, who was an enthusiastic Cambridge
man and college man and Phi Beta man, said with
perfect good nature of the Transcendentalists, that
their utterances seemed to him to be compounded
like the bolts of Jupiter, —

> " Tres imbris torti radios, tres nubis aquosæ
>   Addiderant, rutili tres ignis, et alitis Austri,"

and made this extempore translation : —

> " Three parts were raging fire, and three were whelming water,
>   But three were thirsty cloud, and three were empty wind ! "

Emerson was too young and too modest, and had
too much real regard and respect for Everett, to
make the reply which one thinks of now : " Whatever the bolts were made of, they were thunder-
bolts ; and from Vulcan's time to this time, people
had better stand out from under when a thunder-
bolt is falling." I can see Emerson now, as he
smiled and was silent.

After thirty years people did not say much about
" thirsty cloud " or " empty wind." Emerson was
in the zenith of his fame. He was " the Buddha
of the West," — that is Doctor Holmes's phrase.
He was " the Yankee Plato," — I believe that is
Lowell's. And Phi Beta made amends for any

vague questioning in the past by the enthusiasm with which it received him for the second time.

A queer thing happened on that morning. Emerson had a passion to the last for changing the order of his utterances. He would put the tenth sheet in place of the fifth, and the fifth in place of the fifteenth, up to the issue of the last "extra" of an oration. It was Miss Ellen Emerson, I think, who took upon herself the duty of putting these sheets in order on this occasion, and sewing them so stiffly together that they could not be twitched apart by any sudden movement at the desk. But the fact that they were sewed together was an embarrassment to him. What was worse was that he met his brother, William Emerson, that morning. I think they looked over the address together, and in doing so it happened that Waldo Emerson took William Emerson's glasses and William took Waldo's. Waldo did not discover his error till he stood in the pulpit before the assembly. Worse than either, perhaps, some too careful janitor had carried away the high desk from the pulpit of the church, and had left Emerson, tall and with the wrong spectacles, to read the address far below his eyes. It was not till the first passage of the address was finished that this difficulty of the desk could be rectified; but the whole audience was in sympathy with him, and the little hitch, if one may call it so, which this made seemed only to bring them closer together.

The address will be found in the eighth volume of his works, and will be remembered by every one who heard it; but, on the whole, what impresses me the most in memory is the hearty thoroughness and cordiality of Lowell's congratulations when Emerson turned round after finishing the oration. "*Par nobile fratrum*," as one said; and one felt glad to have seen two such men together on such a day. Lowell himself said of it, a few days later : —

"Emerson's oration was more disjointed than usual even with him. It began nowhere and ended everywhere; and yet, as always with that divine man, it left you feeling that something beautiful had passed that way, something more beautiful than anything else, like the rising and setting of stars. Every possible criticism might have been made on it, except that it was not noble. There was a tone in it that awakened all elevating associations. He boggled, he lost his place, he had to put on his glasses; but it was as if a creature from some fairer world had lost his way in our fogs, and it was our fault and not his. It was chaotic, but it was all such stuff as stars are made of, and you could not help feeling that if you waited awhile all that was nebulous would be hurled into planets, and would assume the mathematical gravity of system. All through it I felt something in me that cried, 'Ha, ha! to the sound of trumpets!'"

On the 9th of July, 1872, Lowell and Mrs. Lowell sailed for Europe, without any plans, as he himself says. They remained abroad two years. They landed in England, but early in the winter he established himself, for six months as it proved, in Paris. They were in a nice little hotel there, where he is still remembered cordially, — the Hotel de France et Lorraine. Here they lived quietly from November to the next summer.

He was in Paris in the last years of M. Thiers. The interests of politics centred on the relations between President Thiers and the Commission of Thirty, — long since, I am afraid, forgotten by this reader. Lowell writes of Thiers's resignation, which closed his long career of public life, "I think it was the egotism of Thiers that overset him rather than any policy he was supposed to have."

Of this sojourn in Paris a near friend of his gives me the following pleasant note : —

"In the little office of the Hotel France et Lorraine, Rue de Beaune, Paris, hangs a fairly good likeness of James Russell Lowell, a large photograph, I think, taken some years before his death. It is, and has been for twenty years and more, the presiding presence of the little sanctum where Madame and Monsieur sit and make out their (very reasonable) bills and count their gains. The hotel is still a most attractive retreat for a certain class of us, who like quiet and comfort without display. Rue de Beaune is a narrow little street leading off the Quai Voltaire, which runs parallel to the Seine. On the opposite shore of the river are the fine buildings of the Tuileries and the Louvre; between flows the steady stream, covered with little steamers, pleasure-boats, bateaux-mouches, tugs. The great Pont-Royal crosses the river, very near Rue de Beaune, to the Rue des Pyramides through the gardens of the Tuileries. It is one of the prettiest

though not the gayest parts of Paris. The bridge
and adjoining streets are crowded with life on foot
and on omnibus; but take one step into Rue de
Beaune, and you find silence, peace, and repose.

"In the winter of 1872–73 Mr. and Mrs. Lowell were living at this modest but well-known hotel,
in its grandest apartments *au premier*. Somewhat
dark and dingy even then, more so now, but neat
and comfortable. The house must be very old. It
is built round a little *cour*, or rather two little
courts; and a winding staircase leads up through
the principal part to the landings of the several
stories. There were two parlors, if I remember,
communicating. The walls were lined with book-
cases, filled with Mr. Lowell's books, and other
furniture of the cosy, comfortable order, when they
established themselves in these congenial quarters.

"Here they lived, read, wrote, talked, enjoyed
themselves. Mr. Lowell was probably writing something of importance, but he had at that time no
public or official business, no pressing engagements.
He was, in fact, doing just what he pleased all the
time. Of course his acquaintance was large in the
American colony and among the best French society of Paris, but I do not think he troubled himself about it much. He delighted in prowling
about the book-stalls which abound in the Quai
Voltaire, where old rubbish in print is displayed
along the parapet of the river in tempting openness,
and where a real book-worm may rummage and find
something really valuable among apparently hopeless stuff. He loved a quiet little dinner (in their

rooms) *à quatre*, or, still better, *à trois*, where the
food was good enough, and the talk excellent; his
cigar came afterwards. Mrs. Lowell, his sympathetic and congenial companion, sat smiling and
interested at such times, like the proper wife of a
good talker, not talking much herself, but showing
in her pleasant, refined face that she appreciated and
enjoyed the fun. Although her health, even then,
was delicate, she was strong enough to share his life
and interests. What they both liked the most was
the quiet of their own fireside, and the unmolested
pursuit of literary pleasures, stimulated by all the
resources of the great city, without any parade, or
the burden of a crowd of engagements. They
might have been any humdrum couple of small
means, passing the winter in the most delightful
city in the world, with all the resources in themselves of wit, intelligence, and mutual affection."

While Lowell was in Europe, King Amadeo, the
Italian sovereign of Spain, abdicated, and the republic of Castelar was born. Lowell was in Venice
in November, 1873, at the time of the Virginius
massacre. But he does not seem to have known,
better than any others of his countrymen in Europe,
how near we were to war with the Spanish republic. Yet in that month Mr. Fish had instructed
Mr. Sickles to break off relations with the Spanish
government unless they could reform their Cuban
administration. "If Spain cannot redress these
outrages, the United States will." Such were the
words in his telegram to Madrid of November 15,
1873.

Lowell had once and again visited his old friend William Story in his residence in Italy. The Storys had visited America in 1865. With Mrs. Lowell he now had an opportunity to visit them in Rome.

Since Mr. Story went to Rome with his wife in 1847 he had been devoting himself to sculpture, but he had never forgotten his American friends; and his light pen kept him in the memory of many of those who did not see his statues. His Cleopatra had won general approval. When the Lowells visited Rome in 1873 Story's Alkestis was new, and Lowell writes of it with genuine pleasure. "It was so pleasant to be able to say frankly, ' You have done something really fine, and which everybody will like.' I wonder whether I shall ever give that pleasure to anybody." This, observe, dear reader, as late as 1874.

Lowell returned to America in the summer of that year, arriving in Elmwood on the Fourth of July.

I myself do not believe that a long residence in Europe is of great help to an American gentleman or lady so far as an estimate of one's own country goes. They are apt to read the London " Times's " view of America, or that contained in Galignani's newspaper, or possibly the Paris edition of the New York " Herald." These utterances from day to day are not encouraging; but if they were true and adequate, one need not complain of discouragement. The truth is, however, that they are not adequate, and therefore they are not true. For one month when I was in Europe in 1873 the daily American dispatch in the "Times" was confined to the fortunes of some wretched Modoc Indians in California, who were hiding among their rocks and were being killed one by one by sharpshooters. For the rest there was practically nothing, — nothing which showed me that brave boys were growing into brave men, that good girls were growing into pure women, that universities and libraries and Chautauquas and summer schools were giving a liberal education to half my country, that merchants were telling the truth and acting the truth, and inventors were renewing the world.

I go a little out of the way to say this, because I observe that Mr. A. Lawrence Lowell, in his admirable notice of his cousin's life, suggests that his stay in Europe in 1872–73 to a certain extent modified his notion with regard to America and American politics. Mr. A. Lawrence Lowell uses the following words : —

"During his stay in Europe Lowell had been distressed at the condition of politics in this country, and annoyed at the expressions of contempt for America it had called forth on the other side of the Atlantic. On his return he was horrified by the lack of indignation at corruption in public life, for the intense party feeling engendered by the war was still too strong to permit independent judgment in politics. He expressed his disgust in a couple of poems in 'The Nation,' called 'The World's Fair' and 'Tempora Mutantur.' The verses were not of a high order of poetry, and at first one regrets that Hosea Biglow did not come out once more to

THE HALL, ELMWOOD

do battle with the spoils system, as he had with the slave power long ago; but the subject was not one that made it possible. Among the archaic sculptures buried on the Acropolis after the sack of Athens by Xerxes, and recently unearthed, is a fragment of a pediment representing Hercules and the Hydra. The hero is on all fours alongside the monster in a cave, a fitting type of the way political corruption must be fought at the present day. The war with slavery, like that of Perseus with the dragon, could be waged on wings with a flashing sword; but the modern reformer must go down on his hands and knees and struggle with reptiles in the dark."

Whether Lowell were right or wrong in thinking that a new wave of Philistinism had overwhelmed the administration of America is of no great importance to us here. I think he was wrong. I think that the American people govern America, and that the intrigues or devices of the men who " run with the machine " are of much less importance than very young people suppose, who read very poor though very conceited weekly newspapers. However that may be, this country has received great advantage from Lowell's determined interference and interaction in our politics in the years which followed his return in 1874. So vigorous were his writings that he was at once recognized as a pure public leader. I have always found that the " machine " is eager to join hands with any man of literary, inventive, or business ability who is willing, as the phrase is, to " go into politics." Certainly this was

so in Lowell's case, and in the autumn of 1876 he
was asked to take a seat in Congress which we call
in Massachusetts the South Middlesex seat. It was
the seat which Edward Everett had captured years
before, in the face of the machine of his time. It
was the seat which William Everett afterwards captured, by fine audacity, although he was not even a
resident in the district. Lowell might have gone
to the Congress of 1877 if he had chosen. He declined the position, estimating correctly his abilities
and inabilities as a member of a legislative body,
" as it seems to me." But, with the same desire to
show that men of character and ability were interested in the Republican party, the nominating convention made him an elector for the presidency.

It was in the famous election after which Hayes
was declared to be President by the electoral commission. I will say in passing that, as acting president of the New England Emigrant Aid Company,
it had been my business to see to the transfer of
two or three thousand voters from the North into
Florida in the years after the rebellion, and that it
was no matter of surprise to me, therefore, that the
electoral commission pronounced that Florida had
given a Republican vote. I believe Florida would
give such a vote to-day, if there were any chance of
its being counted.

When it was clear that the election of Mr. Hayes
would depend on a single ballot in the electoral
college, there were intriguers so mean as to suggest
that possibly Mr. Lowell might be persuaded — I
suppose by considerations which such men under-

stand better than I do — to give a vote for Mr.
Tilden.   Any such hopes as these Mr. Lowell very
promptly suppressed, as such a man can.   That little correspondence, however, called attention to his
name, even in the somewhat dark council chambers
of the people who distrust " them littery fellers."

Fortunately for America also, in all turns of our
politics there has been the same sense of the value
of literature and of the sphere of men of letters
which has given the world about all the good diplomacy which the world has ever had.   Somewhat as
Franklin was sent to France because the French
had heard of him before, quite as Motley was sent
to Vienna because he knew something about history
and could speak the language of Germany, exactly
as Mr. Irving had been sent to Spain as our minister, the new administration made advances to Mr.
Lowell to ask him if he would not represent us at
one of the European courts.

The following notes may be published now, for
the study of annalists, as most of the people who
are referred to are dead : —

(April 13, 1876.)   "What I meant to say was
that if, when the Russian embassy was offered me,
it had been the English instead, I should have hesi-
tated before saying no.   But with the salary cut
down as it is now, I could n't afford to take it, for
I could not support it decently."

(April 19, 1876.)   "I return Mr. Fish's letter.
There is no more chance of their sending me to St.
James's than to the moon, though I might not be
unwilling to go.   On the old salary I might manage,

and it might do my health good. I have little doubt
that it was offered to L. with the understanding
that he would decline. I have not seen him for a
few days. But it is too large a plum for anybody
not 'inside politics.' It is the only mission where
the vernacular sufficeth. Meanwhile, you will be
amused to hear that I am getting inside politics after
a fashion. I shall probably head the delegation
from our ward to the state convention."

Four foreign missions were offered him. He
declined all, but in declining said, perhaps without
much thought, that if they had offered him the
mission to Spain, he would have gone. Mr. Evarts
was Secretary of State, and it may readily be imagined that he was able "to manage it." And so it
was that this professor in Harvard College, who had
kept his eyes so far open that he knew of the existence of Abraham Lincoln in 1860, was appointed to
represent the United States in Spain.

CHAPTER XIII

MR. LOWELL IN SPAIN

THE reader ought to understand that while the Spanish mission has always been spoken of by uninformed people as a somewhat lazy corner in that somewhat old-fashioned salon which takes the name of " Diplomacy," the United States minister in Spain has always been walking amidst hot coals, or explosive friction matches. Some drowsy people, whose principal business in life has been to cut off the coupons from securities which other people had earned for them, waked up with surprise when they learned that this country had at last taken up the gauntlet of war. The United States meant to finish the job which Drake and Burleigh and Howard and Elizabeth left unfinished three centuries ago. But other people were not surprised. If they have cared about the history of the hundred years which have made the United States a nation, — and which have seen ten or twelve changes either of constitution or of dynasty in Spain, — men have known that open questions, some of them of great seriousness, have all the time entangled the diplomatic web which was woven between the two nations.

Into the heritage of these complications Lowell came when — in a pacific time — he presented his

credentials at Madrid. The sovereign then on the
throne was Alfonso XII., and one of Lowell's earli-
est dispatches describes the ceremonies attending
his marriage with Mercedes, the young princess.
The minister of foreign affairs was Don Fernando
Calderon Collantes. The short-lived republic which
began in 1873, on the abdication of Amadeo of
Savoy, had, in its time, given way, and the old
Bourbon family had returned in the person of
Alfonso XII.

In the short period of the republic I happened
to be editing the magazine called "Old and New,"
in Boston. Like most intelligent Americans, I
hoped to see republican government extend itself in
Europe.

I wanted, at all events, that our readers should
know the truth about it. I struck high, as an editor always should do. So I waited on Charles
Francis Adams, the same who had carried through
our negotiations with England in the civil war with
such masterly success. If there ever were a Republican and Democrat, it was he; if there ever were a
person confident in the strength of America, it was
he; and I certainly expected his sympathy in the
cause of the new-born Spanish republic.

I asked him to write our article on Spain and
the new republic. He listened to me with all his
perfect courtesy; and then he advised me — I
might say he bade me — take no stock in the enterprise. I pressed him; I said, "Surely, we want to
extend republican institutions in Europe?" And
he smiled, sadly enough, and said, "Do not expect

anything of Spain, Mr. Hale. *The truth is not in them.*"

In this old Bible axiom of Covenanters and of Puritans is the secret of all the difficulties between England and Spain in Drake's time, between this country and Spain in Jefferson's day, and in each of the crises of negotiation since. Spain and her statesmen really think that a lie well stuck to is as good as the truth. Our representatives do not think so. The difference makes a jar when the neophyte in diplomacy discovers it.

In the unpublished " Pickering correspondence " are some curious memoranda which show what Jeferson thought and planned. Jefferson had seen the real Philip Nolan killed, and nine American companions of his kept in lifelong imprisonment in Mexico because the Spanish government violated its own passports. This all began as early as 1801. In 1825 Mr. Alexander Everett, our minister in Spain, offered the Spanish government one hundred millions for Cuba. Under Mr. Polk's government, twenty years after, the offer was renewed. Mr. Soulé, our minister in Madrid between 1853 and 1855, complicated matters by his personal quarrels. He fought a duel with Turgot, the French minister, and incurred the dislike, naturally enough, of the French government. At a conference of three American foreign ministers at Ostend in 1854, Buchanan, Mason, and himself, Soulé pressed the importance of the annexation of Cuba to the United States, and carried with him both of his coadjutors.

But it is not at all necessary that we should enter

into the details of these complications. The history
of all this diplomacy has been admirably written by
Professor Hart, and is published in " Harper's Magazine" of June, 1898. We should probably have
gone to war with Spain at Mr. Soulé's suggestion,
but that at that moment, in 1854 and 1855, the
weak government of that weakest of men, Franklin
Pierce, was in very hot water at home. The administration had offended the whole North by its
operations in Kansas, and it was no time to ask for
a war which seemed likely to end in the annexation
of another slave State to the Union. Mr. Soulé
was recalled, and some sort of *modus vivendi* was
patched up which carried us through the civil war.
Mr. Lincoln appointed Mr. Koerner as our minister
in Spain, who was succeeded by Mr. John Parker
Hale.

One is glad to say that at this time the drift
of the somewhat wayward movements of Spanish
administration was in our favor. A curious little
anecdote, which I think has never been printed,
illustrates this; and as it has an indirect bearing on
after diplomacy, I will repeat it here. After our
civil war had ground along for nearly three years,
Louis Napoleon, as will be remembered, took a hand
in it. He formed the ingenious plan of uniting
other nations in a change of the international law
governing blockades. The admiralty law of the
world at present extends the jurisdiction of any
nation for one marine league from its shores. If,
therefore, a blockade-runner could get within three
miles of Jamaica, Cuba, or Porto Rico, he was safe

from any interference from our blockading fleet. Napoleon ingeniously proposed that, instead of one league, this limit of local sovereignty should be extended to three leagues from shore. He knew well enough that England would never consent to this change; but he had that audacity which enabled him to persuade the Spanish minister to come into his plan.

Maps of the West Indies are now plenty, and any reader who will look at the position of Cuba, Porto Rico, and the little French islands in the West Indies will see how seriously such an extension of a neutral limit would have hindered the operations of our blockading fleets. All this negotiation was conducted with great secrecy, and orders were sent from Spain to the West Indies, instructing the local authorities there to extend threefold the range of their dominion over the sea. These orders had already gone when Mr. Horatio Perry, our secretary of legation at that time, got wind of this treachery of our ally.

What Mr. Perry did in this issue was wise. He told his wife. She went immediately and told the Duchess of Montpensier, who had none too great love of Louis Napoleon, " the nephew of his uncle," and the occupant of Louis Philippe's throne. She told her sister, the queen. The queen sent at once for Mr. Perry.

He told her what the emperor had done, and what her own ministers had done. I suppose he said, " You are injuring your best friends, — at the solicitation of this intriguer, whom you hate, and who is your worst enemy." The queen said this was the first she had heard of the matter, and she would send for her prime minister.

So she did. And he came. And she asked him if this thing had been done. And he confessed that it had; Her Majesty had signed the order on such or such a day.

" But no one told me what it meant," said poor Isabella. " No one told me that this was a heavy blow to my American allies."

No. No one had told her. The minister explained that as well as he could. If Her Majesty disliked it, he was sorry, but he was too late to help it. Why too late? the queen asked. Because a steamer had gone to the West Indian fleet with the orders which changed one league to three leagues.

Then Queen Isabella spoke the words which, as I count it, were the best words of her life: —

" It is not too late for me to accept your resignations."

And when it came to that, it proved that the Señor Don did not want to resign, and the other Señores Dons did not want to resign, and they found a fast steamer to take out orders rescinding the other orders. And so the Emperor Napoleon got a slap in his face, and so the blockade was maintained for the next year.

And so Spain scored one on her private account with the Washington government, and Isabella II. found one decent thing on the credit side when she stood at the bar of St. Peter or history.

Whoever will refer to the published state papers

will find no reference to this interesting incident. It is the sort of thing they leave out in printing. But you can see that it must have taken place in the autumn of 1863, if you will read between the lines.

As I have said, the intelligent reader of these lines has read Professor Hart's admirable review of the diplomacy of the United States and Spain regarding Cuba for a hundred years ; or, if he has not read it, he had better read it as soon as he can find the " Harper's " for June, 1898. He will learn that in that century there were but two cases of direct interference with the destinies of Cuba, one by President John Quincy Adams in 1826, and one by President Grant in 1875. At the same time he will find that there were filibusters in 1849, 1851, again in the years 1868–78, again in 1884–85, when the American administration gave these filibusters neither aid nor comfort. In 1854 and 1873 there came reasons for war, and they were not regarded. Simply, these references to events of the utmost importance will show the reader what were the traditions of our legation in Madrid when Mr. Lowell arrived there, in August of 1877.

I must have talked with him about the Spanish politics of his time, for I saw him often in London, just before I visited Spain in 1882, and I traveled there with the benefit of his instructions. But I kept no notes of what he said, and I dare not refer any of my own impressions directly to him. For myself in Spain I had only the poor chance which a traveler of forty days has to learn from the daily newspapers, from table-d'hôte talk, and from interviews, too short, with intelligent men of all parties and professions.

I conceived a very high respect for the rank and file of the Spanish people. Ignorant? Yes, if reading and writing are the tests of ignorance, for only one fifth of the population can read their own language. But the people themselves, the average people, as I saw them, seemed to me a very civil, friendly, self-respecting, thoughtful, and industrious people. They were ready to oblige a stranger, and they did not expect a penny or a shilling, as an Englishman or an Irishman does when he has obliged a stranger.

I see that careful students of the position now say that the class of people in administration in Spain, the people who make and unmake ministries and dynasties, are more absolutely separate from what I call the rank and file than anywhere else in the world. I had a suspicion of this when I was in Spain.

At the same time I observed that the circulation of the daily newspapers in Madrid was as great as is that of the papers in Boston, the two cities being near the same size. They were bitter and violent in their satire and in their attacks on each other. I think there were three bright and well-illustrated comic dailies, each with a large colored cartoon. Here, I think, was the tribute to the people who could not read. I suppose that the proportion of people who can read is much larger in Madrid than in the whole nation.

Sagasta was at the helm in 1882, as he is in 1898.

I find that I wrote of him then, " If you trusted the newspapers, you would say that there is only one man in Spain, or possibly two, who wanted Sagasta to stay in, — that this one was Sagasta himself, — that the other was possibly his confidential private secretary. You would say that everybody else was wild to have such an absurd pretender pushed from his throne, and every morning you would be sure that he would fall before the next day, and would be at once forgotten."

But at the same time I wrote, " As it seems to me, Sagasta is one of the ablest men in Europe, and I think the king has as high an opinion of Sagasta as any of us can form. . . . And I think the king is a remarkable young man, and that if he can hold on for five years longer, as he has for the last eight, he will be counted not only as one of the wisest sovereigns in Europe, but as one of the wisest of the nineteenth century."

This, so far as the young king goes, is very strong; it now seems absurd. But one hopes so much from young kings! and this fine fellow — he was that at least — died when he was not thirty-one. The first story any one told you of him, when I was in Spain, was this : that when he was asked to take the crown, after the republic of Castelar had broken down, he said, " Yes, I will come if you wish. Only, when you want me to go, tell me so, and I will go. Remember, all along, that I am the first republican in Europe."

Of the young king, Lowell himself gives his opinion in this anecdote : —

"On Saturday, the 26th [of October, 1878], the king received the felicitations of the diplomatic body. Among other things, he said to me, 'I almost wish he had hit me, I am so tired.' Indeed, his position is a trying one, and I feel sure that if he were allowed more freely to follow his own impulses and to break through the hedge of etiquette which the conservative wing of the restoration have planted between him and his people, his natural qualities of character and temperament would make him popular."

To us in America it is interesting to remember that in the court of this young king, who made so favorable an impression in his short reign of eleven years, was one whom we may call an American lady. That is to say, Madam Calderon, to whom the important charge of the education of his sisters was intrusted, was the wife and afterward the widow of Calderon de la Barca, a distinguished Spanish diplomatist. She was Miss Fanny Inglis, born in Scotland, the granddaughter of Colonel Gardner, of Preston Pans. In her youth she removed to Boston with her sister, Mrs. McLeod, and there was a teacher in her sister's school. She was a very brilliant, conscientious, and agreeable person, and as the wife of Calderon de la Barca when he was Spanish minister to the United States, and afterwards in Mexico, made, as she deserved, a wide circle of friends. She had the charge of this prince as soon as he needed a governess, and of his sisters. The Spanish government showed its appreciation of her services by presenting to her a beautiful home, above the Alhambra, in Granada, where many of her old American friends subsequently visited her. She died in the royal palace at Madrid, in the winter of 1881–82.

Of our legation in Madrid Lowell himself says, in a private note, that the secretary of legation whom he found there says that it is the hardest-worked legation in Europe.

I myself have known personally five or six gentlemen who have held the position, and all of them have given me the same impression. I remember one of these gentlemen told me that he was still at work on a claim which one of our captains had against the Spanish government for interference with his vessel ten years before. The *mañana* policy had dragged the thing along so far. So that in that legation one had to keep in mind the history of half a dozen Spanish dynasties.

At this moment, writing when we are in war with Spain and the plaza of Santiago de Cuba is again historical, it is impossible not to go back a quarter of a century. At that time the governor of Santiago shot, without trial, in that plaza, fifty-four men, most of them American citizens. They had been captured in the Virginius, a filibustering steamer; but according to any law of any nation which pretended to any civilization, they deserved and should have received trial. It was then that Mr. Fish sent to Mr. Sickles, our minister in Spain, the dispatch to which I have referred, "If Spain cannot redress these outrages, the United States will."

Why was Spain let off then? It seems such a

pity now. A short shrift then would have saved
two or three hundred thousand lives which have
been lost in the barbarism of Spanish administration since. Whoever will read the complicated
correspondence of that year will see that General
Grant exercised the utmost forbearance. Spain
was at that moment a republic : what American
wanted to crush a poor little European republic
which could hardly hold its head above water?
The gentlemen in authority in Madrid descended to
the most pathetic petitions that they might be excused, — if only this time we would let them off
from what they deserved, no such barbarism should
ever be tolerated again. The minister of foreign
affairs would come over himself to the American
legation to plead a postponement of justice. At
the end Spain promised to pension the families of
the people her viceroy had murdered. So General
Grant gave way, and when, four years after, Mr.
Lowell arrived, it was his duty to show that we had
forgiven, and were trying to forget.

Of the foreign dispatches from our ministers, our
government means to print only that which is
wholly harmless in future diplomacy. There is,
therefore, but little of Lowell's in print which bears
upon the questions most interesting now. But
once and again he says that, when the Spanish
government had paid something which it owed, the
foreign minister would beg that notice might be
taken of it, as showing their friendly wish to do
their duty when they could.

Here is a little scrap, unimportant enough in

itself, but fairly pathetic now in its open confession by a Spanish minister of the power for reserve or deception which such a minister has — or thinks he has.

In inclosing it Lowell says : —

(April 2, 1878.) " The interpellation of General Salamanca may either indicate that there is some doubt in the mind of the party to which he belongs as to the complete pacification of Cuba, or that he thought it a good topic about which to ask a question that might be embarrassing to the ministry. The answer of Señor Canovas admits, as you will see, that armed resistance still exists, and seems to imply even more than it admits. I am not sure that it would be safe to draw any inference from this, as Señor Canovas has, from the first, shown great discretion and reserve with regard to the recent events and Cuba." . . .

(Inclosure.) "Señor Canovas. . . . For the rest, the government, in fact, knows concerning the internal condition of Cuba, concerning the preliminaries of capitulation, and concerning other points, more than it has hitherto had occasion to lay before the members of this body. But this is not what I said before; I did not say that the government had not more information on this than it had communicated to Congress, for if that were the case, I should not have had occasion to suggest what I have suggested. . . . Concerning what preceded the capitulation, concerning the capitulation itself, concerning what the government expects after the capitulation, concerning what it believes will result from the capitulation, concerning the possible length of the war, concerning the reasons the government has for hoping what it may hope and fearing what it may fear, — the government has its own knowledge, and thinks it inopportune, at present, to enter into discussion. But concerning the fact of the forces which have submitted, concerning what remains to be done in the way of pacification, the government has no kind of secret."

Señor Canovas was the minister who was murdered last year.

With such cares, and in such difficult surroundings, Lowell spent the close of 1877 and the years 1879 and 1880. He was then summoned, very unexpectedly, to transfer his residence to London as United States minister to England.

In the mean time, with his astonishing power of work, he not only attended curiously well to the work of the legation, but had devoted himself sedulously to the study of the Spanish language and literature. His private letters have the most amusing and interesting references to such studies. When he was presented to the king, he made his speech in English, the king answered him in Spanish, then came forward and exchanged a few compliments in French. But very soon it appears that he was determined not to be dependent on any interpreter, or on the accomplishment of any of the foreign officers with whom he had to do. "I am turned schoolboy again, and have a master over me once more, — a most agreeable man, Don Herminegildo Giner de los Rios, who comes to me every morning at nine o'clock for an hour. We talk

Spanish together (he does n't understand a word of English), and I work hard at translation and the like." And again : " This morning I wrote a note to one of the papers here, in which my teacher found only a single word to change. Was n't that pretty well for a boy of my standing ? "

This he writes to his daughter and to Miss Norton : " I like the Spaniards, and find much that is only too congenial in their genius for to-morrow. I am working now at Spanish as I used to work at Old French, — that is, all the time, and with all my might. I mean to know it better than they do themselves, which is not saying much. . . . This is the course of my day : get up at eight ; from nine, sometimes till eleven, my Spanish professor ; at eleven breakfast, at twelve to the legation, at three home again and a cup of chocolate, then read the paper and write Spanish till a quarter to seven, at seven dinner, and at eight drive in an open carriage in the Prado till ten, to bed twelve to one."

He writes to a friend in 1878 that he found that the minister of state for foreign affairs sometimes smoked a pipe in the secrecy of home. " I was sure he must be blistering his tongue with Spanish mundungus, and sent him a package of mine. He writes to say, ' It is the best I ever smoked in my life ; I had no idea there was anything so good.' So I sent him yesterday ten more packages, and have promised to keep his pipe full for so long as I am here."

Of his own work in his vocation as diplomatist he says : " I am beginning to feel handier in my new

trade, but I had a hard row to hoe at first. All
alone, without a human being I had ever seen before
in my life, and with unaccustomed duties, feeling as
if I were beset with snares on every hand, obliged
to carry on the greater part of my business in a
strange tongue, it was rather trying for a man with
so sympathetic and sensitive a temperament as mine,
and I don't much wonder the gout came upon me
like an armed man. Three attacks in five months!
But now I begin to take things more easily. Still,
I don't like the business much, and feel that I am
wasting my time. Nearly all I have to do neither
enlists my sympathies much nor makes any call on
my better faculties. I feel, however, as if I were
learning something, and I dare say I shall find I
have when I get back to my own chimney-corner
again. I like the Spaniards, with whom I find many
natural sympathies in my own nature, and who have
had a vast deal of injustice done them by this com-
mercial generation. They are still Orientals to a
degree one has to live among them to believe. But
I think they are getting on. The difficulty is that
they don't care about many things that we are fools
enough to care about, and the balance in the ledger
is not so entirely satisfactory to them as a standard
of morality as to some more advanced nations. They
employ inferior races (as the Romans did) to do
their intellectual drudgery for them, their political
economy, scholarship, history, and the like. But
they are advancing even on these lines, and one of
these days — But I won't prophesy. Suffice it that
they have plenty of brains, if ever they should con-

descend so far from their *hidalguia* as to turn them
to advantage. They get a good deal out of life at
a cheap rate, and are not far from wisdom, if the
old Greek philosophers who used to be held up to
us as an example knew anything about the matter."

It must have been a joy to Mr. Evarts, in the Department of State at home, to read Lowell's dispatches when they came. It is reserved for those
who have the inner keys to the inner bureau of the
department to read them all; but here are some
passages which have been printed in the government
reports, — because harmless, — which make one understand why he was sent to England when there
was a vacancy there : —

(February 6, 1878.) " In these days of newspaper enterprise, when everything that happens ought
to happen, or might have happened is reported by
telegraph to all quarters of the world, the slow-going
dispatch-bag can hardly be expected to bring anything very fresh or interesting in regard to a public
ceremonial which, though intended for political
effect, had little political significance. The next
morning frames of fireworks are not inspiring, unless to the moralist; and Madrid is already quarreling over the cost and mismanagement of a show for
the tickets to which it was quarreling a week ago."

. . . " Whoever has seen the breasts of the pea-
santry fringed with charms older than Carthage and
relics as old as Rome, and those of the upper classes
plastered with decorations, will not expect Spain to
become conscious of the nineteenth century and
ready to welcome it in a day."

. . . " A nation which has had too much glory
and too little good housekeeping." . . .

Here is the pathetic account of the young queen's
death. She was the first wife of Alfonso XII.
The present queen regent (the Austrian) is the
second : —

(July 3, 1878.) " Groups gathered and talked in
undertone. About the palace there was a silent
crowd day and night, and there could be no question that the sorrow was universal and profound.
On the last day I was at the palace just when the
poor girl was dying. As I crossed the great inte-
rior courtyard, which was perfectly empty, I was
startled by a dull roar not unlike that of vehicles in
a great city. It was reverberated and multiplied by
the huge cavern of the palace court. At first I
could see nothing that accounted for it, but presently found that the arched corridors all around
the square were filled, both on the ground floor and
the first story, with an anxious crowd, whose eager
questions and answers, though subdued to the utmost, produced the strange thunder I had heard.
It almost seemed for a moment as if the palace itself
had become vocal.

. . . " The match was certainly not popular, nor
did the bride call forth any marks of public sympathy. The position of the young queen was difficult
and delicate, demanding more than common tact and
discretion to make it even tenable, much more influential. On the day of her death the difference was
immense. Sorrow and sympathy were in every heart
and on every face. By her good temper, good

sense, and womanly virtues, the girl of seventeen had not only endeared herself to those immediately about her, but had become an important factor in the destiny of Spain.   I know very well what divinity doth hedge royal personages, and how truly legendary they become even during their lives, but it is no exaggeration to say that she had made herself an element of the public welfare, and that her death is a national calamity.   Had she lived, she would have given stability to the throne of her husband, over whom her influence was wholly for good. She was not beautiful, but the cordial simplicity of her manner, the grace of her bearing, her fine eyes, and the youth and purity of her face gave her a charm that mere beauty never attains."

We may call this dispatch the first version of his sonnet : —

DEATH OF QUEEN MERCEDES.

Hers all that Earth could promise or bestow,
Youth, Beauty, Love, a crown, the beckoning years,
Lids never wet, unless with joyous tears,
A life remote from every sordid woe,
And by a nation's swelled to lordlier flow.
What lurking-place, thought we, for doubts or fears
When, the day's swan, she swam along the cheers
Of the Alcalá, five happy months ago ?
The guns were shouting Io Hymen then
That, on her birthday, now denounce her doom ;
The same white steeds that tossed their scorn of men
To-day as proudly drag her to the tomb.
Grim jest of fate !   Yet who dare call it blind,
Knowing what life is, what our humankind ?

Early in 1880 Lowell received unexpectedly a request from the Department of State that he

would represent the nation in England. He writes
to his daughter the following interesting account of
his transfer : —

" Day before yesterday I was startled with a cipher
telegram. My first thought was, ' Row in Cuba !
I shall have no end of bother ! ' It turned out to
be this : ' President has nominated you to England
[this President was Hayes]. He regards it as essential to the public service that you should accept and
make your personal arrangements to repair to London as early as may be. Your friends whom I have
conferred with concur in this view.' "

Then Mr. Lowell says that he was afraid of its
effect on Mrs. Lowell, who was recovering from a
long and desperate illness; but she was pleased,
and began to contrive how he might accept. He
goes on, " I answered, ' Feel highly honored by
President's confidence. Could accept if allowed
two months' delay. Impossible to move or leave my
wife sooner.' "

When I was in Madrid I heard this story. The
two months' delay did not prove necessary. Just at
this juncture poor Mrs. Lowell was confined to her
bed, and had been for some time. It happened that
a candle set fire to the bed-curtains. The attend-
ants fell on their knees to implore the assistance of
the Holy Mother, but Mrs. Lowell sprang up and
herself took the direction of the best methods for
extinguishing the flames. So soon as nurses and
others could be brought into shape, it proved that
the adventure had not been an injury to their mis-
tress, but rather an advantage. The doctor was

summoned at once, and within a very short time
was able to say that Mrs. Lowell could be removed
with care and sent by steamer to England. Mr.
Lowell was said to have telegraphed at once to
Washington that he could transfer his residence
immediately, as he was asked to do. Accordingly,
by a well-contrived and convenient arrangement,
the invalid was taken by rail to the sea, thence by
steamer to England, and arrived there, with her
husband, with no unfavorable results to her health.

In this sketch of Mr. Lowell's life in Madrid I
have not attempted, and indeed have not been able,
to introduce even the names of the friends in whose
society Mr. Lowell took pleasure while in Spain.
But American scholars, and indeed the scholars of
the world, have been so much indebted to Señor
Don Pascual de Gayangos, whose recent death has
been so widely regretted, that I ought not to close
this chapter without referring to him.

This gentleman is another of the distinguished
men born in 1809. In early life he studied in
France. He visited England and married an English lady. When he was but twenty-two years of
age he held a subordinate place in the administration at Madrid. He returned to England while yet
a young man, and resided there. Articles of his
will be found in the " Edinburgh Review " at that
time. After the Oriental Society published a translation by him of " Almakkari's History," he was
appointed professor of Arabic in Madrid. He had
studied Arabic under De Sacy.

Every American student in Spain for the last

half-century has been indebted to his courtesy, and, I may say, to his authority in Spain. As one of the humblest of those students I am glad to express their obligation to him.

His only daughter, a charming lady, married Don Juan Riano, a distinguished archæologist, who is, I think, now in the diplomatic service of the Spanish government. Her son, Don Pascual's grandson, is secretary to the queen, or has been so lately. All of them were near friends of Lowell.

CHAPTER XIV

MR. LOWELL had declined the suggestion that he should go to England when Mr. Hayes's administration came in. But one need not say that when he now determined to go to England, he went there with the pleasure with which every one of our race visits what we still call the "mother country." His ancestry, his education, and the studies in which he had taken the very broadest interest, all made him love England.

He was an American through and through, and, as his own celebrated address, which I shall speak of again, showed to the world, he comprehended democracy in its possibilities, in its future, and in its present better than almost any man of his time. He was better able to show it to the leaders of the feudal communities in which he lived, better than any other American who could have been chosen. For all this, — it would be better to say because of this, — he went and came in England with that sort of delight which Mr. Edward Everett fifty years before described so well : —

"An American looks at Westminster Abbey and Stratford-on-Avon with an enthusiasm which the Englishman laughs at as a sort of provincial rawness."

This enthusiasm of the American in England is
so genuine that one may not speak with adequate
contempt of the sneers with which banished Irishmen ridiculed it, when they had occasion to speak
of Mr. Lowell while he stayed in the home of his
ancestors.

As minister to England Mr. Lowell rendered
essential service to his country. His firmness, se-
renity, courtesy, and diligence enabled him to keep
on the best terms with the members of the English
cabinet with whom he had to do. He was to a
remarkable degree, as we shall see, a favorite with
all classes of the English people. He satisfied the
administration of President Hayes, who sent him.
He did not satisfy the more talkative leaders of
the Irish-Americans, who, to use a happy phrase of
his, were like an actor who "takes alternately the
characters of a pair of twins who are never seen on
the stage simultaneously."

But nobody could have satisfied them. They
were in a false position, — so false that even diplomacy of the old fashion could not have satisfied it.
No man can serve two masters, and no man can be
a citizen of two nations at the same time. So those
gentlemen found out who, while, as Irishmen, they
pressed the Irish people to revolt, fell back under
the ægis of America when they got into trouble.
For the others, for those who had really made themselves Americans, and meant to remain such, Mr.
Lowell was more than the advocate. He was their
fearless guardian. And in such guardianship he was
always successful. Here, let it be said, first and

last, he knew nothing of the morals of that diplomacy of the older fashion. He might have directed a dispatch wrong, so that Lord Granville should read what was meant for Mr. Evarts, and Mr. Evarts what was meant for Lord Granville, and no harm would have been done. That was his way, — as, be it said, it is the way of gentlemen, and, in general, of our national negotiations.

At the same time Lowell made friends in England among all classes of people. For a generation the line of American ministers had generally been good. From time to time we sent one or two fools there, usually to get them out of the way of home aspirations and ambitions. But Mr. Everett, Mr. Lawrence, Mr. Bancroft, Mr. Adams, Mr. Welsh, and Mr. Motley were all conscientious, intelligent gentlemen, who really were as much interested in English history and English literature as Englishmen were, and "really, you know, they spoke English very well, with almost no accent, you know."

Diplomacy, and the whole business of ambassadory, is, in fact, about as much out of place in our time as chain mail is, or as orders of precedence are. But people of sense try to make a new diplomacy in which each nation can approach, not the government of the other, but the people. Mr. Lowell, who could think on his feet, who could speak well in public, who had always something to say, and who, indeed, liked to say it, had a real "calling" in this line. In his English stay he made several public speeches which did more good than any "state paper," so called, could have done.

In private society he was a favorite, as he was everywhere. In 1882 somebody told me in London the story of an invitation which Lord Granville, the foreign minister, had sent him. Lord Granville, in a friendly note, asked him to dinner, saying at the same time that he knew how foolish it was to give such short notice "to the most engaged man in London." Lowell replied that "the most engaged man is glad to dine with the most engaging."

Also, London is an excellent place in which to study, and to learn without studying. And, from the first, Lowell enjoyed London and England. Mrs. Lowell was able sometimes to receive her friends, and even to bear the fatigue of a reception at court, and of presenting to the queen American ladies who visited London. She made herself most welcome in the circle, not large, whom she was able to meet in that way. The delicacy of her health, however, prevented her husband from attempting the more public social functions of hospitality, of that kind that consists mostly in calling people together to dinners or evening parties. But he was, all the same, cordial to all comers from his own nation, ready and successful in promoting their object, while, as has been said, he was at ease among all classes in England. His holidays, if we may call them so, were spent privately in visits with friends, and for six or seven summers in Whitby, — the Whitby of "Marmion," in the north of England, — a place of which he was very fond.

He was presented and began on his formal duties in the winter of 1881–82. His stay in England

WHITBY

lasted until June 10, 1885. Mrs. Lowell had died in February of that year.

The first important matter in his negotiations was connected with the Irish disaffection. Most general readers to-day will have forgotten that an insurrection, or plan of insurrection, attributed to the Fenian organization, had disturbed Ireland and frightened England not long before. The name Fenian was taken from Fein McCoil, the *Fin*-gal of Ossian. Lowell, who could never resist a pun which had any sense in it, called the Fenians *Fai-néants*, which, as it proved, was fair enough, except that they and theirs kept their English masters in alarm. I was talking with a Liberal in England in May, 1873, and he said, "Why, if you had landed in Ireland, you would have been in jail by this time." I asked what was the matter with me. He said that my crush hat and my broad-toed shoes would have convicted me. Now the shoes had been bought in Bristol, only three days before, and I said so. "Bristol? were they? Well, they knew you were a Yankee." That is to say, any one who looked like an outsider had to run his chances with the Irish constables of the time.

Among others who were less fortunate than I, Henry George was arrested. He was as innocent as I, and was at once released, with proper apologies.

The view which Lowell took, and the dilemma in which his Irish clients acted, and even went to prison, are well explained in a dispatch from which I will make a few short extracts. The whole collection of dispatches shows the extreme unwillingness of Lord Granville to give offense in America : —

March 14, 1882.   (Received March 27.)

In concluding this dispatch I may be permitted to add that I have had repeated assurances from the highest authority that there would be great reluctance in arresting a naturalized citizen of the United States, were he known to be such.   But it is seldom known, and those already arrested have acted in all respects as if they were Irishmen, sometimes engaged in trade, sometimes in farming, and sometimes filling positions in the local government.   This, I think, is illustrated by a phrase in one of Mr. Hart's letters, to the effect that he never called himself an American.   He endeavors, it is true, in a subsequent letter, to explain this away as meaning American born; but it is obviously absurd that a man living in his native village should need to make any such explanation. Naturalized Irishmen seem entirely to misconceive the process through which they have passed in assuming American citizenship, looking upon themselves as Irishmen who have acquired a right to American protection, rather than as Americans who have renounced a claim to Irish nationality.

Simply, the view he sustained is that which he laid down in two letters written to Mr. Barrows, to be read to one of these prisoners, from which here are a few extracts.   They embody briefly the established policy of our government : —

" The principles upon which I have based my action in all cases of applications to me from naturalized citizens now imprisoned in Ireland under the 'Coercion' Act are those upon which our government has acted, and in case of need would act again. I think it important that all such persons should be made to understand distinctly that they cannot be Irishmen and Americans at the same time, as they now seem to suppose, and that they are subject to the operation of the laws of the country in which they choose to live."

In another letter he says : —

"If British subjects are being arrested for no more illegal acts than those which the prisoner is charged with having committed, or of the intention to commit which he is justly suspected, it seems that, however arbitrary and despotic we may consider the 'Coercion' Act to be, we are, nevertheless, bound to submit in silence to the action taken under it by the authorities even against our own fellow citizens.

"It should be observed that this act is a law of the British Parliament, the legitimate source and final arbiter of all law in these realms, and that, as it would be manifestly futile to ask the government here to make an exception on behalf of an American who had brought himself within the provisions of any law thus sanctioned, so it would be manifestly unbecoming in a diplomatic representative, unless by express direction of his superiors, to enter upon an argument with the government to which he is accredited as to the policy of such a law or the necessarily arbitrary nature of its enforcement."

That neither he nor the American government

was hard on the "suspects" appears from several letters, of which this illustrates the tenor: —

TO OUR CONSUL AT LIMERICK.

You will please see without delay John McInerny and Patrick Slattery, suspects claiming to be American citizens and confined in Limerick jail, and say to each of them that " in case he should be liberated you have authority to pay him forty pounds sterling for his passage to the United States," for which sum you may draw upon me at sight.

This sort of correspondence ended in May, 1882. The following letter was practically the end of it.

TO MR. FRELINGHUYSEN.

Meanwhile it is nearly certain that all the suspects, except those charged with crimes of violence, will be very shortly set at liberty, thus rendering nugatory the most effective argument in favor of disorder and resistance to the law.

To turn from such correspondence to his frank relations with the people of England, it is interesting to see how readily he accepted the modern theory of American diplomacy. This makes the foreign minister the representative not only of the administration, but of every individual among the people. It recognizes the people as indeed the sovereign. In this view, for instance, the American minister has to place rightly the inquiries of every person in the United States who thinks that there is a fortune waiting for him in the custody of the Court of Chancery. In such cases the American citizen addresses "his minister" directly. On a large scale the foreign minister has the same sort of correspondence as the " domestic minister " at home, of whose daily mail half is made up of the inquiries of people who have not an encyclopædia, a directory, or a dictionary, or, having them, find it more easy to address the clergyman whose name they first see in the newspaper. They turn to him to ask what was the origin of the Aryan race, or what is meant by the fourth estate.

The reader who has not delved into the diplomatic correspondence does not readily conceive of the range of subjects which thus come under the attention of an American minister abroad, in the present habit, which unites the old diplomacy and the formality of old centuries with the hustling end-of-the-century practice, in which every citizen enjoys the attention of the minister. In Lowell's case subjects as various as the burial of John Howard Payne's body, the foot-and-mouth disease in cattle, the theological instruction in the schools of Bulgaria, the assisted emigration to America of paupers from Ireland, and the nationality of Patrick O'Donnell occupy one year's correspondence. Those of us who think that the old diplomacy is as much outside modern life as chain mail is, or the quintessences of old chemistry, might well take the body of John Howard Payne as an object-lesson.

(1) John Howard Payne wrote " Home Sweet Home."

(2) 1852. He died and was buried in Tunis, where he represented the United States.

(3) 1882. Mr. W. W. Corcoran thought he should like to bury his body in America, with a proper monument.

(4) October. Mr. Corcoran asks the coöperation of Mr. Frelinghuysen, our Secretary of State.

(5) October. Mr. Frelinghuysen writes to Mr. Lowell to ask for the intervention of the British government, because we have no representative in Tunis.

(6) November. Mr. Lowell writes to Lord Granville, the English foreign secretary.

(7) November. Lord Granville bids Mr. Lister attend to it.

(8) November. Mr. Lister writes to Mr. Reade and to Mr. Lowell to say he has done so.

(9) January, 1883. Mr. Lowell writes to Mr. Frelinghuysen to say how far they have all got.

(10) January. Mr. Frelinghuysen writes to Mr. Lowell to ask that the body may be sent to Marseilles.

(11) January. Mr. Lowell writes this to Lord Granville.

(12) January. Lord Granville telegraphs to Mr. Reade at Tunis, and writes to Mr. Lowell that he has done so.

Meanwhile they become impatient at Washington, and the Assistant Secretary telegraphs : —

January 2. "Have you received news from Tunis relative to Payne's remains?"

Mr. Lowell telegraphs back, much as if it were the answer in the "Forty Thieves:" —

January 3. "Not yet, but presently."

On the same day, apparently, or

January 1. Lord Granville receives a telegram from Tunis, to say that all has been done, and that the remains would be shipped to Marseilles.

January 6. Mr. Reade explains all to Lord Granville, and also to Mr. Taylor. Every one was present at the disinterment who should have been.

January 12. Mr. Lowell thanks Lord Granville and Mr. Currie and Mr. Reade and all the other officials.

February 9. Mr. Frelinghuysen asks Mr. Lowell to thank everybody; and it is to be presumed he does so.

Very well. This required a good deal of red tape. But it was very nice of Mr. Corcoran to put a monument to the poet of "Home," and somebody must do something.

It is interesting to see how wide are the consequences of such courtesies, and how important they may be.

Lowell really wanted to serve the American people, and any intelligent question addressed to him found a courteous and intelligent reply. It would not be difficult to give a hundred instances, and if any of the diplomats of to-day sometimes groan under the burden of such correspondence, let me encourage them by copying an autograph letter of his which a friend has sent to me this morning. A public-spirited gentleman in Minnesota had determined that there should be a school of forestry in that State. He knew there was such a school in India

at Dehradun.　He wanted the report of that school,
and so he sent to the United States legation in
London to ask for it.　Here is Mr. Lowell's reply,
and it is interesting to know from Mr. Andrews that
it was of real service in the establishment of the first
school of forestry of America : —

LEGATION OF THE UNITED STATES,
LONDON, March 10, 1882.

DEAR SIR, — On receiving your letter of the 17th
of February I at once wrote to Lord Harrington,
who the next day sent me the report, which I now
have the pleasure of forwarding to you, and especially if it helps you in awakening public opinion to
the conservation of our forests ere it be too late.　I
foresee a time when our game and forest laws will
be Draconian in proportion to their present culpable
laxity.

Faithfully yours,

J. R. LOWELL.

Hon. C. C. ANDREWS.

A foreign minister of America once said to me
that Diplomacy meant Society, and Society Diplomacy.　He meant that the important things are
done in personal conversation between man and
man, as they sip their coffee after a dinner-party,
perhaps.　The conclusions thus arrived at get themselves put into form afterwards in dispatches.　In
this view of diplomacy it was fortunate for all parties
that Mr. Lowell and Lord Granville were the correspondents who had American affairs in hand, from
such " emblems " as the American flag on Lord

Mayor's Day round to the nationality of Mr. O'Connor. Fortunate, because the two liked each other.

Lord Granville's term of office as foreign secretary was almost the same as Lowell's as American minister. Granville came in with the Gladstone ministry in April, 1882, and he went out of office with them in 1885. Lowell's personal relations with him were those of great intimacy. He not only regarded Lord Granville with cordial respect, but knew him as an intimate friend. In 1886 he visited Lord Granville at Holmbury, at a time when Mr. Gladstone was also visiting there. "I saw Gladstone the other day, and he was as buoyant (*boy*ant) as when I stayed with him at Holmbury, just before he started for Scotland. I think the Fates are with him, and that the Tories will have to take up Home Rule where he left it."

Lord Granville was very young when he entered Parliament, as Mr. Levison Gower, member for Morpeth. He is said to have regretted the change of work in the House of Lords when he became Lord Granville. In 1859, when he was not forty-five years old, the queen asked him to form a cabinet, and in 1880 she consulted him with the same view again; but he did not become chief of the ministry at either time. He served under Lord Palmerston and under Mr. Gladstone, as he had done under Lord John Russell. He was, while he lived, the leader of the Liberals in the House of Lords, always in the minority, whatever the policy of the hour, but always cordial, amiable, and conciliatory. On Gladstone's retirement in 1878 he was spoken of as the real leader of the Liberal party. It is said of him that he always kept a friend who was once a friend, — that he was willing to yield small points in controversy rather than to keep a quarrel in existence, and always " sacrificed his personal interests to those of his party."

Such a man is a friend whom one likes to have ; and such a character gives point to Lowell's joke, which I have cited, which calls him the most engaging man in London. I remember with pleasure the first time I saw him. He was acting as chancellor of the University of London — as long ago as 1873. He was presenting the diplomas to those who had passed the examinations for degrees of that university. This means that two or three hundred young men, from all parts of Great Britain, were presented to him, by the heads of perhaps twenty different colleges, to receive this distinction. Now, such a formality may be merely a function, as stupid to see as stupid to go through. In this case there was genuine personal contact between the chancellor and the neophyte. As each one of those youths, proud or timid, came up, and as Lord Granville gave the diploma to each, he detained him, for the moment, by some personal word or inquiry, — such as you could guess the man who was entering life would always remember. With such a man Lowell would be sure to be on sympathetic terms. And I suppose they met each other, or were in close correspondence, almost every day in the " season."

But Lowell was not only the minister from the

people; he was a messenger to the people. And he had sense enough and historical knowledge enough to know that since there has been an America on the western side of the Atlantic, the people of England — the rank and file — have been in sympathy with the thought and feeling and purposes of that American people. When my brother Charles was in London in 1863, and the English government was acting, on the whole, as badly as it dared toward the United States, a member of the cabinet said to him one day, " The clubs are against you, Mr. Hale, but the people of England are with you." This was true then; it was true in the American Revolution; it was true in Cromwell's time, — he has no title which is more sure than that of the " Friend of New England." The same thing is true to-day.

Now, Lowell never said to himself, " Go to, I will address myself to the people of Great Britain," or, " The people of Great Britain is one thing, and the clubs of London another." But because he was the man he was, he was always glad to meet the people and the men of the people, and let them really know what America is. It is not the America of interviewers, of excursionists, of *nouveaux riches* millionaires, or of namby-pamby philanthropists attendant on international conventions. These are the individuals whom the people of England are most apt to see. But the people of America, at home, have wider interests than theirs, and affairs more important than they have. Lowell felt this in every fibre of his life, and if the Workingmen's College in London, or some public meeting at Birmingham, or a

Coleridge monument, gave him a chance to give to the people of England his notion of what the people of America are, and have in hand, why, he was most glad to do so.

This is no place in which to describe or discuss his successes as a public speaker in England. It was a matter of course that, as soon as he spoke once, whoever heard him would be glad to hear him again; and he must have had proposals without number for his assistance in public dinners, at the unveiling of monuments, and in addresses of wider range and of more permanent importance.

In the two volumes of admirable memoirs of English life which Mr. Smalley has published, one chapter is given quite in detail to the description of Lowell's remarkable welcome among Englishmen of every degree. In that chapter, which I suppose is made from one or two letters published at the time, Mr. Smalley quotes "The Spectator," as saying that Englishmen, whether they knew Mr. Lowell or not, looked on him as a personal friend.

Of all the various addresses which contributed, each in its place, to his reputation as a public speaker, that which I have alluded to, which was delivered at Birmingham, on "Democracy," is the most remarkable. It has, indeed, become a classic. It deserves its reputation; and it undoubtedly states with careful accuracy Lowell's foundation feeling as to the institutions of this country, and what may be expected if democracy is fairly understood and fairly applied. No one who was familiar with him or with his letters, or had really studied his more serious poems, will regard any of the utterances in this great address as being new. They were the words of a careful scholar who was born under favorable circumstances in the midst of democracy admirably well applied. His training was all the better because the original people of Massachusetts are, so to speak, democratic in their origin and in the habit of their thought, without having formed many abstract theories on the subject, and being always, indeed, quite indifferent as to what the speculative theory might be.

An American minister abroad must not be often or long absent from his post. But there are methods by which four fortnights of permitted absence may be added together, and your outing taken at once. In some way Lowell was thus free for a tour through the Continent to Italy in the autumn of 1881. In Italy he and Story and Mr. Richard Dana met. Dana was at the Wells School with him when they were little boys, and in Italy they had that most agreeable of companions, Mr. John W. Field. Dana died the next winter, and Lowell writes to Field, " The lesson for us is to close up " — " if a year or two older than I, he belonged more immediately to my own set, and I had known him life long."

In the summer of 1882, returning from Spain to America, I spent a month in London. I told Lowell one day that I was one of the " round-the-world " correspondents of the Murray Dictionary, and that I wanted to call on Dr. Murray. He said he had been trying to do the same thing, and proposed to take me, — an invitation which, of course, I accepted.

The reader ought to know that the Oxford Dictionary, now nearly half finished, was undertaken forty-one years ago, — as early as 1857. The first suggestion was made by Dean Trench, and, at the vote of the Philological Society, several hundred readers agreed to contribute notes made in their reading of English books, for the materials of such a dictionary. After twenty-one years some specimen pages were prepared from the notes collected by such readers, and submitted by Dr. Murray to the Clarendon Press in Oxford. Dr. Murray is now known through the English-speaking world for his charge of this magnificent work, which, I think, men will always call "Murray's Dictionary."

The directors of the Clarendon Press agreed to assume the immense cost and charge of publication, and in 1888 the first volume of the great series, now as far forward as H and I, appeared. The contributors' names make a very valuable list of people interested in good English. And the volumes thus far published are the treasury to which all other dictionary-makers rush as their great storehouse of materials.

For the purpose of systematic coöperation, each reader was prepared with formal printed blanks. Each of these was to have, as far as his special reading showed, the history of one word. That word in large letters was the head of the completed blank. The reader is not necessarily an authority in language. He is a scout or truffle-dog who brings the result of his explorations to the authorities for comparison with other results.

Mill Hill, where the dictionary was then — shall I say manufactured? — is about ten miles, more or less, from the house which Lowell lived in. As we entered the cab which was to take us, he said that he should bid the cabby carry us through the back of the Park, a region which I had never seen. I have been amused since to see how many traveling Americans can say the same thing. Lowell evidently knew its turns and corners and bosks and deserts well. Ragged, barefoot boys were playing cricket in their improvised way with the most primitive of tools, such as they had constructed from the spoils of the streets. No policeman bade them leave the place, no sign intimated that they were to keep off the grass; an admirable loafers' paradise for the real children of the public, such as there is not in our tidy Common in Boston, and such as I never saw in the Central Park of New York. It was pleasant to see how thoroughly at home Lowell was there. To such retreats in London he alludes again and again in his letters: " I have only to walk a hundred yards from my door to be in Hyde Park, where, and in Kensington Gardens, I can tread on green turf and hear the thrushes sing all winter. . . . As for the climate, it suits me better than any I have ever lived in."

Spare a moment, dear reader, to find what greeted us at the Dictionary House. I doubt if they have yet invented any such name as Apotheka, or Powerhouse, or Granary. As why should they, seeing this is the only such house in the world? A circular house of corrugated iron, originally built for a church, I believe, perhaps fifty feet in diameter, perhaps twenty-five feet high, lighted from the top. It reminded me, at the instant, of the great reading-room of the British Museum, though not so large. Here was Dr. Murray, the distinguished director, at work with his staff of gentlemen and ladies. Of course he was delighted to see Lowell on the spot, and in the simplest and kindest way he showed us the method of the work.

Every day's mail brought to this curious temple of language its new tribute to the history of the English tongue. The slips which I have tried to describe come from Cranberry Centre and Big Lick, from Edinburgh and from Hongkong. Once a month each of the thousand or more readers mails his budgets, so there would be every day a new parcel to be assorted; and we were ready for them at Mill Hill. Here were twenty or thirty thousand pamphlet-boxes into which these slips were at once sorted. The boxes were arranged in alphabetical order, beginning with that which held the slips of the title word A, and only ending, say, with box 33,333, with the box of ZYX — if there be so convenient a word in the English language.

All which I describe in this detail, because I should be glad if the reader will imagine the gay, bright, wise, and instructive talk which followed — oh, for an hour, perhaps hours — between Dr. Murray, the first authority as to English words, and Lowell, the authority most to be relied on as to the language of New England. It was not far from the time when Lowell told the Oxford gentlemen at a public dinner that they spoke English almost as well as their cousins in America. No, I do not remember what were the words these gentlemen discussed. But each was as eager as the other. Was it "doddered" or "daddock"? I do not know. "Miss Mary, will you have the goodness to bring us 'dodder'?" And Miss Mary puts up a light ladder to her D O shelf and returns with the pasteboard box which has five and twenty uses of "dodder" between the days of Wiclif and Besant, and the two scholars dissect and discuss. You would think that Lowell had never thought of anything else. And yet it is the same Lowell who in a quiet corner of Mrs. Leo Hunter's to-night will be discussing with Lord Granville the amount and quality of the theology which the Great Powers shall permit in the secondary schools of Bulgaria!

I must not try to give any account in detail of the company of literary men and women whom Lowell found in London. Two careful and interesting papers by Mr. Bowker, published in "Harper's" in 1888 and 1889, are well worth the reader's attention. From these papers I have made some lists of people, almost any one of whom you would be glad to have met, who worked their pens in London, or printed their books there, in those years. Mr. Bowker himself, as the English representative of "Harper's," was living there, and his personal notes of these people are valuable as they are entertaining. Of novelists alone he gives a list in which are these names : —

Wilkie Collins, Richard Doddridge Blackmore, Miss Braddon (Mrs. Maxwell), Dinah M. Craik, Thomas Hardy, Walter Besant, James Payn, David Christie Murray, Henry Rider Haggard, Robert Louis Stevenson, Clark Russell.

Take those ten names only, and you say, as a lady once said to me, " Any one of them would make the fortune of a reception." But Mr. Bowker's next ten do not pale in comparison : —

F. W. Robinson, George Macdonald, George Meredith, W. E. Norris, Mrs. Ritchie (Anne Thackeray), Mrs. Oliphant, Amelia Blandford Edwards, Mrs. Elizabeth Lynn Linton, Miss Yonge, and Mrs. Macquoid. Observe, these twenty are only some of the novelists.

Among other men and women of letters, there are Tennyson, Browning, Hughes, Bailey, both Morrises, Domett, Taylor, Mallock, Kinglake, our dear old Martin Tupper, Stephen, Walter H. Pater, Addington Symonds, Swinburne, Buchanan, the Rossettis, Jean Ingelow, Owen Meredith, Matthew Arnold, Austin Dobson, Alfred Austin, Coventry Patmore, Gerald Massey, Max Müller, Spencer, Tyndall and Huxley, Lubbock, and the two Cardinals, Manning and Newman. Other clergyman are Farrar, Haweis, and Spurgeon. Besides these, among men who have done more than write books, there are, in Mr. Bowker's lists, Froude, McCarthy, and Lecky to represent history, and Dr. Smith, king of dictionaries. Smiles, the self-help man, Colvin, and Hamilton are others.

I think I may say that Lowell knew personally all

THOMAS HUGHES

the more distinguished of the persons in these very interesting groups before he left London. He formed some very tender friendships among them, and in the collection of his letters none are more affectionate, none are more entertaining, than are those to his English friends. Besides those named in the lists above there are ladies, — Mrs. Stephen, the Misses Lawrence, Mrs. Clifford; and Gordon, Du Maurier, Lord Dufferin, are mentioned as people with whom he was in pleasant relations. Lady Lyttelton was a most intimate friend of Mr. and Mrs. Lowell.

Among other intimate friends, Judge Hughes and Mrs. Hughes. Dr. Hughes, as every one knows, had been a guest at Elmwood, and Mr. Lowell during his residence as our minister in England, and in his visits there afterwards, would have thought a summer wasted indeed if he had not received the welcome of these dear friends.

With the election of Mr. Cleveland in the autumn of 1884 Lowell knew that his stay in England would come to a close. For ten or fifteen years, indeed, he had been in public antagonism to Mr. Blaine, and he would never have served under him as President in the English legation. More than this, however, Mrs. Lowell died in the spring of 1885, unexpectedly, of course, for death is always unexpected. "We had taken it for granted together that she would outlive me, and that would have been best." How many a man and woman have had to say something like that!

She had been an invalid, with critical ups and

downs. But her unfailing sympathy for him and his work had never yielded, and those who remember him in the closest intimacies of London life always speak of her with tenderness. She was almost always shut up at home, and he was everywhere, among people of all sorts and conditions. But the very difference of their lives when they were parted seemed to make their companionship more tender when they were at home.

Of his departure from England, his cousin, Mr. Abbott Lawrence Lowell, says, with truth : —

" But his usefulness as a minister far transcended the import of any specific questions that arose. It was his personal presence there, winning the respect and admiration of the English for all that is best in America, that was most valuable. Among the many surprises in Mr. Lowell's life none is perhaps greater than that, after writing so bitterly about Mason and Slidell, he should have been instrumental in soothing the irritation between England and America that arose out of the civil war ; but such is the case, and it is not too much to say that he did more than any one else towards removing the prejudice which the upper classes in England had for the United States." And Mr. Smalley at the time wrote from London : —

" The announcement of Mr. Lowell's recall gives rise to many expressions of regret and good will besides those which appear in the newspapers. Nor is the expression of good will a new thing. His writings, his speeches, and his public services had brought him so close to all English-speaking people that their feeling toward him was one of affection ;

in short, there were ninety millions who would rejoice in any good fortune that befell him, and sympathize with him in trouble. The solicitude to know whether he was to remain minister has been general. ' Will President Cleveland keep Mr. Lowell in London ? ' is the question which every American in London has been asked over and over again since last November ; perhaps twice a day on an average. And when the inquiring Briton was told that Mr. Lowell would have to go, the next question generally was, ' What, then, did the President mean by Civil Service Reform ? ' "

What indeed?

CHAPTER XV

HOME AGAIN

LOWELL landed in America again in June, 1885. It was nearly seven years since he left us on his way to Spain. And these were seven years which had changed, in a thousand regards, the conditions of his old American home.

In August, 1891, he died, seventy-two years old,— six years after this return. Of these years we have in his letters a record of pathetic interest, and every one who knew him and who loved him will say that of the seven decades of life — to which more than once he alludes — he never seemed more cheerful and companionable and cordial and wise than in the seventh. "And young," he would often have said himself. He discusses old age and its coming in his letters to near friends, — yet perhaps more than is wise, certainly more than is necessary. But once and again he tells his correspondent that he is as young as a boy. He signs himself, in writing to Gilder, "Giacopo il Rigiovinato." And he writes out : —

From the Universal Eavesdropper :

ANECDOTE OF JAMES RUSSELL LOWELL.

Passing along the Edgeware Road with a friend two years ago, their eyes were attracted by a sign

with this inscription, "Hospital for Incurable Children." Turning to his companion, with that genial
smile for which he is remarkable, Lowell said quietly,
"There's where they'll send *me* one of these days."

But, all the same, seven years of Europe had
changed Elmwood and Cambridge and Harvard College and New England and America and the world.
In a way, of course, Lowell knew this as well as
any man. He knew it better than most men knew
it. And there were a good many sad things in
his arrival, as there must be after seven years. So
many deaths of old friends! So many changes in
the daily life of the people around him! And he,
almost without a vocation; obliged to establish his
new avocations!

Some years before this, Mr. Lothrop Motley, in
all the triumph of his well-earned success after the
publication of his first volumes of history, came back
to his old home — shall I say for a holiday? I do
not know but that he meant to reside here. Not
many months after he arrived, however, he told me,
to my surprise, that he was going back to Europe.
He was going to work in Holland on the archives
again; to continue his great historical enterprise. I
need not say that I expressed my regret that he was
to leave us so soon. But he replied, almost sadly,
that there was no place here in Boston for a man
who was not at work: "You ought to hang out a
long pendant from one of the forts in the harbor to
the other, and write on it, 'No admittance except on
business.'" This was fatally true then of Boston;
it is near the truth now.

And Lowell was no longer a diplomatist; nor had he any special abuses to reform; he had no regular lectures to deliver; he had no wife with whom to talk and read and make dinner linger long, and breakfast and lunch. He was in a changed world, and for that world had to prepare himself.

Perhaps it is as well to say that Boston also was changed; the Boston of 1885 was not the Boston of 1838. The late Mr. Amos Adams Lawrence said to me, not long before his death, that his father used to say that in the beginning of the century Boston was governed by the great national merchants: such men as "Billy Gray," one of whose ships discovered the Columbia River; or as Colonel Perkins, who handled the trade of the East in the spirit in which a great artist composes a great picture; or as William Tudor, who supplied ice to the tropics, and when a winter failed him in New England, sent his schooners up into Baffin's Bay to cut ice from the icebergs.

Mr. Lawrence said that when this sort of men gave up the government of Boston, it fell into the hands of the great mechanics: such men as developed the quarries at Quincy; as built Bunker Hill Monument, and in later days have built the Mechanics' Hall, have united Boston with San Francisco and all the Pacific coast by rail. And then, he said, the government of Boston passed into the hands which hold it now, — into the hands of the distillers and brewers and retailers of liquor.

So far as the incident or accident of administration goes, this bitter satire is true; and it expresses one detail of the change between the Boston of the middle of this century and the Boston to which Lowell returned in June of 1885. Now, such a change affects social order; it affects conversation; in spite of you, it affects literature. Thus it affects philanthropy. The Boston of 1840 really believed that a visible City of God could be established here by the forces which it had at command. It was very hard in 1885 to make the Boston of that year believe any such thing.

But Lowell was no pessimist. He was proud of his home, and I think you would not have caught him in expressing in public any such contrast as I have ventured upon in these lines. On the other hand, the letters which Mr. Norton has published in his charming volume confirm entirely the impression which Lowell's old friends received from him: that he was glad, so glad, to be at home; that he had much to do in picking up his dropped stitches; and that he liked nothing better than to renew the old associations. It was, so to speak, unfortunate that he could not at once return to Elmwood. In fact, he did not establish himself there for three years. But, on the other hand, at Southborough, five-and-twenty miles from Boston, where he lived at the home of Mrs. Burnett, his daughter, he had a beautiful country around him, and, what was always a pleasure to him, the exploration of new scenery.

I asked a near friend of his if Lowell were the least bit wilted after his return. "Wilted? I should say not a bit. Bored? yes; worried, a little. But," he added, as I should do myself, "the last talk I had with him, or rather listened to, I shall never forget."

He spent the winter of 1889 in Boston with his dear sister, Mrs. Putnam, from whose recollections I was able to give the charming account which he furnished to us of his childhood for the first pages of this series. We have lost her from this world since those pages were first printed. And he was, of course, near his old friends and kindred : Dr. Holmes, John Holmes, all the Saturday Club, Dr. Howe, Charles Norton, — his intimate and tender friendship with whom was one of the great blessings of his life. These were all around him. But there was no Longfellow, no Appleton, no Emerson, no Agassiz, no Dana, no Page; Story was in Europe.

For occupation, he had just as many opportunities for public speaking as he chose to use. He had to prepare for the press the uniform edition of his works, both in prose and in poetry. It seems to me that he was too fastidious and rigid in this work. I think he left out a good deal which ought to have been preserved there. And this makes it certain that the little side-scraps which the newspapers preserved, or such as linger in some else forgotten magazine, will be regarded as among the treasures of collectors. More than that, many a boy and many a girl will owe to some such scraps inspirations which will last them through life. He occasionally published a poem, and occasionally delivered an address or lecture. But he took better care of himself than in the old days. There was no such crisis before the country as had engaged him then;

WILLIAM PAGE

and, in a way, it may be said that he enjoyed the
literary leisure which he deserved.

He was, alas! at many periods during these six
years a very sad sufferer from sickness. There is
something very pathetic in the manly way in which
he alludes to such suffering. From no indulgence
of his own, he was a victim of hereditary gout; and
you find in the letters allusions to attacks which
kept him in agony, which sometimes lasted for six
weeks in succession. Then the attack would end
instantly; and Lowell would write in the strain
which has been referred to, as if he were a boy
again, skating on Fresh Pond or tracing up Beaver
Brook to its sources.

Simply, he would not annoy his friends by talking
about his pains. If he could cheer them up by
writing of his recovery, he would do so.

I remember that on the first visit I made him
after he was reëstablished at Elmwood, when I con-
gratulated him because he was at home again, he
said, with a smile still, " Yes, it is very nice to be
here; but the old house is full of ghosts." Of
course it was. His father and mother were no
longer living; Mrs. Burnett, who was with him
there, was the only one of his children who had survived; and the circle of his brothers and sisters had
been sadly diminished. He and his brother, Robert
Lowell, died in the same year. Still, he was here
with his own books; he had the old college library
under his lee, and he had old friends close at hand.
Once or twice in his letters of those days he goes
into some review of his own literary endeavor. Cer-

tainly he had reason to be proud of it. Certainly he was not too proud; and I think he did have a feeling of satisfaction that his neighbors and his country appreciated the motive with which he had worked and the real success which he had attained.

As the great address at Birmingham sums up conveniently the political principles which governed his life, whether in literature or in diplomacy, so the address at the quarter-millennium celebration of Harvard College at Cambridge may be said to present a summary of such theories as he had formed on education, and of his hopes and his fears for the future of education. There are two or three aphorisms there which I think will be apt to be quoted fifty years hence, perhaps, as they are not quoted to-day. In the midst of a hundred or more of gentlemen who had served with him in the college he had the courage to say, "Harvard has as yet developed no great educator; for we imported Agassiz."

On the 30th of April, 1889, there was a magnificent festival in the city of New York, at which he spoke. It is already forgotten by the people of that city and of the country, but at the moment it engaged universal attention. It was the celebration of the centennial of the establishment of the United States as a nation; the centennial of the birth of the Constitution; of the inauguration of Washington. It was, of course, the fit occasion for the expression of the people's gratitude for the blessings which have followed on the establishment of the federal Constitution.

For this celebration the most admirable arrange-

MR. LOWELL IN HIS STUDY AT ELMWOOD

Taken in the spring of 1891

ments were made in New York by the committee
which had taken the matter in hand. In the evening a banquet was served at the Metropolitan Opera-
House, and many of the most distinguished speakers
in the country had gladly accepted the invitation to
be present. Among them Lowell naturally was one.
But to those who listened, it seemed as if all these
great men were in a sort awed by the greatness of
the occasion. His address, perhaps because so carefully prepared, was for the purpose no better than
any of the others. They could not help it. Every
man who spoke was asking himself how his speech
would read in the year 1989. There was no spon-
taneity; instead of it there was decorum and consideration, the determination to think wisely, and
none of the eloquence which " belongs to the man
and the occasion." For hour after hour the patient
stream of considerate commonplace flowed on, till
at two in the morning the new President of the
United States made the closing speech. The expectation of this address, and that alone, had held
the great audience together. He was probably the
only man who had not had a chance " to make any
preparation." He had gone through the day alive
with the feeling of the day, drinking in its inspirations; and with such preparation as six hours at the
dinner-table would give him, he rose to say what
the day had taught him. He made one of the most
magnificent addresses to which I have ever listened.
He led with him from height to height an audience
jaded and tired by the dignity of lawyers, the dex-
terity of politicians, and the commonplace of schol-

ars. In fifteen minutes he had established his own reputation as a great public orator among the thousand men who were fortunate enough to hear him.

And yet, such is the satire of what we call history that, because the other speeches had been written out and could be sent to the journals, — because even a New York morning newspaper has to go to press at some time, — this absolutely extemporaneous speech of the one man who proved himself equal to the occasion did not get itself reported in any adequate form, and will never go down into history. There is, however, no danger that any of the other addresses of that great ceremonial will be read at the end of the hundred years.

His cousin says that Mr. Lowell was chiefly occupied by his addresses and other prose essays in the first years after his return, but that he wrote a few poems. Most of these will be found in the " Atlantic." For the Lowell Institute he prepared a course of lectures on the old English dramatists, which have been published since his death. Of his addresses he printed but few, but the address on " The Independent in Politics," which he delivered in 1888 before the New York Reform Club, was printed by that club.

Of his Cambridge life after his return to Elmwood his cousin writes : " The house was haunted by sad memories, but at least he was once more among his books. The library, which filled the two rooms on the ground floor to the left of the front door, had been constantly growing, and during his stay in Europe he had bought rare works with

ROOM ADJOINING THE LIBRARY, ELMWOOD

the intention of leaving them to Harvard College. Here he would sit when sad or unwell and read Calderon, the ' Nightingale in the Study,' in whom he always found a solace. Except for occasional attacks of the gout, his life had been singularly free from sickness, but he had been at home only a few months when he was taken ill, and, after the struggle of a strong man to keep up as long as possible, he was forced to go to bed. In a few days his condition became so serious that the physicians feared he would not live; but he rallied, and, although too weak to go to England, as he had planned, he appeared to be comparatively well. When taken sick, he had been preparing a new edition of his works, the only full collection that had ever been made, and he had the satisfaction of publishing it soon after his recovery. This was the last literary work he was destined to do, and it rounded off fitly his career as a man of letters."

Of these six years perhaps his friends remember his conversation most. Like other great men and good men, he did not insist on choosing the subject for conversation himself, but adapted himself to the wishes and notions of the people around him. His memory was so absolute, his fancy was so free, and his experience so wide that he seemed as much at home in one subject as in another. But when he had quite his own way among a circle of people more or less interested in books or literature, the talk was quite sure to drift round into some discussion of etymologies, of dialect, or of the change of habit which comes in as one or two centuries go by.

And when his curiosity was once excited about a
word — as I said when I was speaking of his talk
with Mr. Murray — he would hold on to that word
as a genealogist holds on to the biography of a great-
grandmother of whom he only knows half the name.
Here are one or two passages from notes which illustrate what I mean : "I used to know some about
Pennsylvania Dutch, but forget their names." "I
wish I could have studied the Western lingo more,
for it has colored our national speech most." "I
think perhaps W. P. Garrison might put you on the
track of something about the Southern *patois*."

"Pitch into the abuse of 'will' and 'shall,'
'would' and 'should;' when we were boys, no
New Englander was capable of confounding them.
I am expecting a statute saying that a murderer
'*will* be hanged by the neck till he *is* dead.' Alas
the day!" And again, "*Daddock* I knew, but
never met it alive; *dodder*, for a tree whose wood
is beginning to grow pulpy with decay, I have heard,
and the two words may be cousins. The latter,
however, I believe to be a modern importation."
Murray and the dictionaries confirm his quick guess
between the relation of one of these words to the
other.

We have a fine American proverb, "Get the
best." In later years I have tried to make some
Western State adopt it for its state seal. I have
never seen it in any earlier use than in one of Lowell's pleasant letters describing a canoe voyage in
Maine; and I wrote to him rather late in his life
to ask him if he were the inventor of the phrase.

It has been adopted, as the reader may be apt to remember, by the authors of Webster's Dictionary, and is a sort of trade-mark to their useful volumes. I am sorry to say that Lowell himself did not remember whether he had picked it up in conversation, or whether he coined it in its present form. For myself, I like to associate it with him.

I find, as I said, I am always reading with pleasure his estimate of his own work in the close of his life. It seems to me to be free from mock modesty on the one hand, as it is from vanity on the other. He seems to me to be as indifferent about style as I think a man ought to be. If a man knows he is well dressed, he had better not recall his last conversation with his tailor; he had better go and come and do his duty. Other people may say about the dress what they choose. In Lowell's self-criticism, if one may call it so, you see the same frankness and unconsciousness, the same freedom from conceit of any kind, which you see in those early expressions which have been cited as illustrations of his boyhood and his youth. If he had said what he wanted to, he knew he had. If he had failed, he knew that. But it seemed to him almost of course that if a man knew what he wanted to say he should be able to say it.

One wishes that this unconsciousness of method could work itself into the minds of literary men more often and more thoroughly. Let a man eat his dinner and let him enjoy it, but do not let the guests discuss the difference between the taste of red pepper and of black pepper. It is as true in literature as everywhere else that the life is more than meat, and the body than raiment. There will probably be sophists and critics and fencing-masters and dancing-masters in all phases of society. They will certainly give much pleasure to each other, and perhaps they will give pleasure to the world; but it may be doubted whether they will be of much use to anybody. I suppose Grant enjoyed a dress parade when he saw it well done, but when they asked Grant how long it took to make a light infantryman, he said, " About half an hour." Let us remember this as we listen, a little bored, to what people have to tell us about style.

There are some curious discussions as to the places and the duties of prose and of poetry; what you had better say in prose, what you had better say in verse. But I am disposed to think that such discussions with him were merely matters of amusement or possible speculation. Everybody who is really familiar with Lowell's writing will remember many passages where the prose may be said to be the translation of his own poetry, or the poetry to be the translation of his own prose. And with such training as his, with such absolute command of language, with his accurate ear and perfect sense of rhythm, it would be of course that he should " lisp in numbers, for the numbers came."

To the very end of his life, his conversation, and his daily walk indeed, were swayed by the extreme tenderness for the feelings of others which his sister noticed when he was a little boy. He would not give pain if he could help it. He would go so much

11ᵗʰ nov: 1890.

Dear Edward,

M. Guizot asked me "how
long do you think the American Republic
will endure?" My answer was, "So long
as the ideas of its founders continue to
be dominant." I quoted this in an
address before the New York Reform Club
1888. Of course I condensed it. In my
conversation with Guizot, I naturally
explained that by "ideas" I meant also
the traditions of their race in government
and morals.

                    Faithfully yours

                         J R Lowell.

Rᵈ Dᵣ Hale.

MR. LOWELL TO DR. HALE

more than halfway in trying to help the person who
was next him that he would permit himself to be
bored, really without knowing that he was bored.
He would overestimate, as good men and great men
will, the abilities of those with whom he had to do.
So his geese were sometimes swans, as Mr. Emerson's were, and those of other lovers of mankind.

His letters are never more interesting than in
these closing years; and, as I have suggested, the
fun of his conversation sparkled as brightly and
happily as it ever did. Mr. Smalley, in an amusing
passage, has described his ultra-Americanism in
England. A pretty Englishwoman said, "Mr.
Hawthorne has insulted us all by saying that all
English women are fat; but while Mr. Lowell is
in the room I do not dare say that all American
women are lean." When Lowell came home he
would take pleasure in snubbing the Anglomaniacs
who are sometimes found in New England, who
want to show by their pronunciation or the choice
of their words that they have crossed the ocean. I
think that every one who is still living, of the little
dinner-party where he tortured one of these younger
men, will remember the fun of his attacks. This
was one of the men whom you run against every
now and then, who thought he must say "Brum-
magem" because Englishmen said so a hundred
years ago; and on this occasion he was taking pains
to pronounce the word "clerk" as if it rhymed
with "lark," — "as she is spoken in England, you
know!" Lowell just pounced upon him as an
eagle might pounce on a lark, to ask why he did so,

why, if it were our fashion to pronounce the word
" as she is spelled," we might not do so, whether on
the whole this were not the old pronunciation, and
so on, and so on.

Never was anything more absurd than the idea
which the Irish sympathizers took up, that a residence in London had spoiled his fondness for the
old idioms and the other old home ways.   Indeed, I
think his stay in Southborough was specially pleasant to him because he learned in another part of
Middlesex County how to renew some of those
studies of " Early America " which he had begun
before he knew in Cambridge.

As one turns over the volume of his letters, he
finds traces of the fancies which shot themselves in
a wayward fashion into his conversation.   One of
the fads of his later life was the taking up of the
notion which we generally refer to Lord Beacons-
field, that almost everything remarkable in modern
life may be traced back, later or earlier, to a Hebrew
origin.   He would discourse at length on the
Hebrew traits in Browning, and he affected to have
discovered the line of genealogy where, a century
or two ago, a streak of the blood of Abraham came
into the lines of the Brownings.   He was quite sure
— I am sorry to say I have forgotten how — that he
had a line of Jewish blood himself, a line which he
could trace out somewhere this side of the times of
Ivanhoe.   Then there was the hereditary descent of
his mother's family from the Hebrides, which has
been referred to.   The Spences were of Traill origin, — his brother Robert carried the Traill name.

And Lowell liked to think that he had in his make-up
something of the element which in a Lochiel you
would call second-sight. Sometimes he alludes to
that in his letters; he has only to shut his eyes, he
says, and he can see all the people whom he has
known, whom he wants to see, and carry on his conversation with them. I have already said that when
I painfully worked through the poems of James
Russell, our James Russell's great-grandfather, rendering that homage to the shade of that poet which
no one else has rendered for a hundred years, I had
to remind myself that he, alas! had no second-sight,
and that he differed from his great-grandson precisely in this, that he was not of Norna's blood and
could not work Norna's miracles.

One of the men of letters whose impressions of
such a life every one is glad to read writes to me of
Lowell's work: "Mr. Lowell excelled at once in original and critical work, thus giving the lie to the
sneer that a critic is a person who has failed as a
creator. Both as a poet and an essayist he revealed
himself as a genuine cosmopolitan. He had the wisdom of the scholar and the horse sense of the man
of the world. He was equally at home in the splen-
did realm of the imagination and in the prosaic
domain of hard facts; and it may be said of him,
as Macaulay said of Bunyan, that he gave to the
abstract the interest of the concrete. As a satirist
and humorist he produced in the 'Biglow Papers' a
work which is unique in our literature. He was not
given to moralizing; his was as far as possible from
being a dull didactic brain; but all to which he put

his pen was wholesome and in the best sense stimu-
lating, free from morbidness and that pessimism of

> 'John P.
> Robinson, he'

who declared that

> 'They did n't know everythin' down in Judee.'"

In one of Lowell's letters written to England after
his return he says that in America they had invented
a new torture while he was away, in the shape of
calling upon authors to read their own works aloud
for the benefit of charities. I am always grateful
to this form of torture when it brings as agreeable
compensation as I remember on an occasion when
we were both reading, I think, for the pleasure of an
audience which had contributed to the purchase of
the Longfellow Park at Cambridge. For this gave
me the pleasure of talking to Lowell for the two
hours while the "entertainment" lasted, as we sat
upon the stage in the Boston Museum. It is rather
a curious thing, to a person as little used to a stage
as I am, to find how wholly the footlights separate
you, not simply from the personal touch of the people in the audience, but from them, until it comes
to be your turn to address them. Even at a public
dinner, when you sit by some agreeable person, you
have not exactly the chance for conversation with
him which you have when both of you are in mediæval chairs dug out from the property-room, and reading is going on quite in front of you which you may
attend to or not, as you both choose. Of course the
fortune of a charity was made, if Lowell were willing
to read poetry or prose which he had written.

As the reader remembers, he lectured again in Boston in one or two full courses to large audiences at the Lowell Institute. He did not absolutely refuse calls from distant cities, but I think traveling became somewhat a burden to him, and after he was once in Elmwood, the associations of the old books and the old life were so pleasant that it was more difficult to draw him away from home.

For his summer holiday, however, he could run across the ocean and visit his English friends in the country, or go back to his pleasant Whitby surroundings. Whitby had for him a particular charm, and one really wishes that he had been in the mood at some time to make a monograph on Whitby, so interesting are some of the references which he makes to it in his letters.

"I am really at Whitby, whither I have been every summer but 1885 for the last six years. This will tell you how much I like it. A very primitive place it is, and the manners and ways of its people much like those of New England. The people with whom I lodge, but for accent, might be of Ashfield. It is a wonderfully picturesque place, with the bleaching bones of its Abbey standing aloof on the bluff and dominating the country for leagues. Once, they say, the monks were lords as far as they could see. The skeleton of the Abbey still lords it over the landscape, which was certainly one of the richest possessions they had, for there never was finer. Sea and moor, hill and dale; sea dotted with purple sails and white (fancy mixes a little in the purple, perhaps); moors flushed with heather in blossom, and fields yellow with corn, and the dark heaps of trees in every valley blabbing the secret of the stream that fain would hide to escape being the drudge of man."

We shall find this "hiding of the stream" again. "I know not why wind has replaced water for grinding; and the huge water-wheels green with moss and motionless give one a sense of repose after toil that to a lazy man like me is full of comfort." "I wish you could see the 'yards,' steep flights of stone steps hurrying down from the west cliff and the east, between which the river whose name I can never remember crawls into the sea." The river appears to have been the Esk River, which Lochinvar swam where there was no ford.

A year afterwards Lowell writes from Whitby: "I am rather lame to-day, because I walked too much and over very rough paths yesterday. But how could I help it? For I will not give in to old age. The clouds were hanging ominously in the northwest, and soon it began to rain in a haphazard kind of way, as a musician who lodges over one lets his fingers idle among the keys before he settles down to the serious business of torture. So it went on drowsily, but with telling effects of damp, till we reached Falling Foss, which we saw as a sketch in water-colors, and which was very pretty.

"Thunderstorms loitered about over the valley like 'Arries on a Bank Holiday, at a loss what to do with their leisure, but ducking us now and then by way of showing their good humor. However, there were parentheses of sunshine, and on the whole it was very beautiful."

Again, the next year, in 1889, he says: "I was received with enthusiasm by the Misses Galilee, the landladies; they vow they will never let my rooms so long as there is any chance of my coming. I like it as much as ever. I never weary of the view from my window; the Abbey says to me, 'The best of us get a little shaky at last, and there get to be gaps in our walls.' And then the churchyard adds, 'But you have no notion what good beds there are at my inn —.' The mill runs no longer, but the stream does, down through a leafy gorge in little cascades and swirls and quiet pools with skyscapes in them, and seems happy in its holiday." We shall come to this "happy holiday" again. Will the reader observe that it is of a series of summers spent in this charming retirement at Whitby, that we hear people speak who talk of his summers in England as if the grand society he had met there had spoiled him for America.

One cannot read Lowell for five minutes without seeing how large his life was, and how little he was fettered by the commonplace gyves of space or time or flesh or sense. He never preaches as Dr. Young would do, or Mr. Tupper, or Satan Montgomery. But, all the same, he is living in the larger life, and so are you if he calls you into his company. Writing to Miss Norton, he says: —

"I don't care where the notion of immortality came from. . . . It is there, and I mean to hold it fast. Suppose we don't know. How much *do* we know, after all? . . . The last time I was ill, I lost all consciousness of my flesh. I was dispersed through space in some inconceivable fashion and mixed with the Milky Way. . . . Yet the very fact that I had a confused consciousness all the while of the Milky Way as something to be mingled with, proved that I was there as much an individual as ever.

" There is something in the flesh that is superior to the flesh, something that can in finer moments abolish matter and pain. And it is to this we must cling. . . .

" . . . I think the evolutionists will have to make a fetich of their protoplasm before long. Such a mush seems to me a poor substitute for the rock of ages, by which I understand a certain set of higher instincts which mankind have found solid under all weathers."

If I am writing for those who have read Lowell carefully and loyally, they know that he knew that "the human race is the individual of which different men and women are separate cells or organs." They know that he knew that " honor, truth, and justice are not provincialisms of this little world," but belong to the life and language of the universe. They know that he knew that he belonged to the universe and was the infinite child of the infinite God. He says sometimes in joke that he hates to go to church. I am afraid that most men who could preach as well as he would say the same thing with the chances of the ordinary religious service. But he also says, " If Dr. Donne or Jeremy Taylor, or even Dr. South, were the preacher, perhaps " —

As it happens, I recollect no expressions of his

more enthusiastic than those in which he described public services of religion. His mother had belonged to the Church of England, and his love for the Prayer Book was associated with his earliest recollections of her.

For the rest, I am sure I should be most sorry to have any one think that a man of his large, religious nature, who lived in the eternities, could be satisfied with the average ecclesiastical function of to-day.

It was a disappointment to him that his health forbade one more visit to his dear Whitby, which he had proposed for the summer of 1890. On the last day of his last visit there, as I suppose, he wrote the beautiful poem, not so well known as it should be, with which I will close this series of reminiscences. He wrote it happily, and he liked it.

It begins with a gay description of the flow and joyous dash of young life. As time passes on, the lively brook is held back by dams sometimes; it is set to work to feed mankind, or to help men somehow; it is pent in and almost prisoned. But not for always. Why should not his brook burst its bonds and leap and plash and sparkle as happily as when it was born?

I print this poem because the circumstances of its composition and publication prevented its insertion in what are generally spoken of as the complete editions edited by himself. He says to his daughter, in speaking of it, "A poem got itself written at Whitby which seems to be not altogether bad; and this intense activity of the brain has the same effect as exercise on my body, and somehow braces up the whole machine." It is a pleasure to feel that he read this beautiful poem himself with something of the satisfaction which every one will find in it. And it is impossible that it should not suggest the conditions of his own closing life. "My Brook," he calls it. And one need not run back to the memories of "Beaver Brook" to fancy the walk or the ride in which some mountain brook in the North Riding renewed the old Cambridge experiences. The charming brook of his youth, gay and joyous, had passed through one and another channel of hard work and of close discipline; but, as he says, there was no reason why, as he and his brook came nearer to the ocean, there should not be the same joy and freedom that there was when he and his brook began on life.

Just after he had written this charming poem — better than that, just when he liked it — it happened that he received an earnest request from that excellent friend of literature, Mr. Robert Bonner, asking him to send something which he might print. On the impulse of the moment Lowell sent this poem. Mr. Bonner kept it for illustration. He illustrated it beautifully, and it appeared before the world fifteen months after, at Christmas of the year 1890, in the New York "Ledger." By the courtesy of Mr. Bonner's sons, I am able to print it all — as the fit close of these papers. I could not otherwise have given so charming a review by the poet of his own life and his eternal hopes.

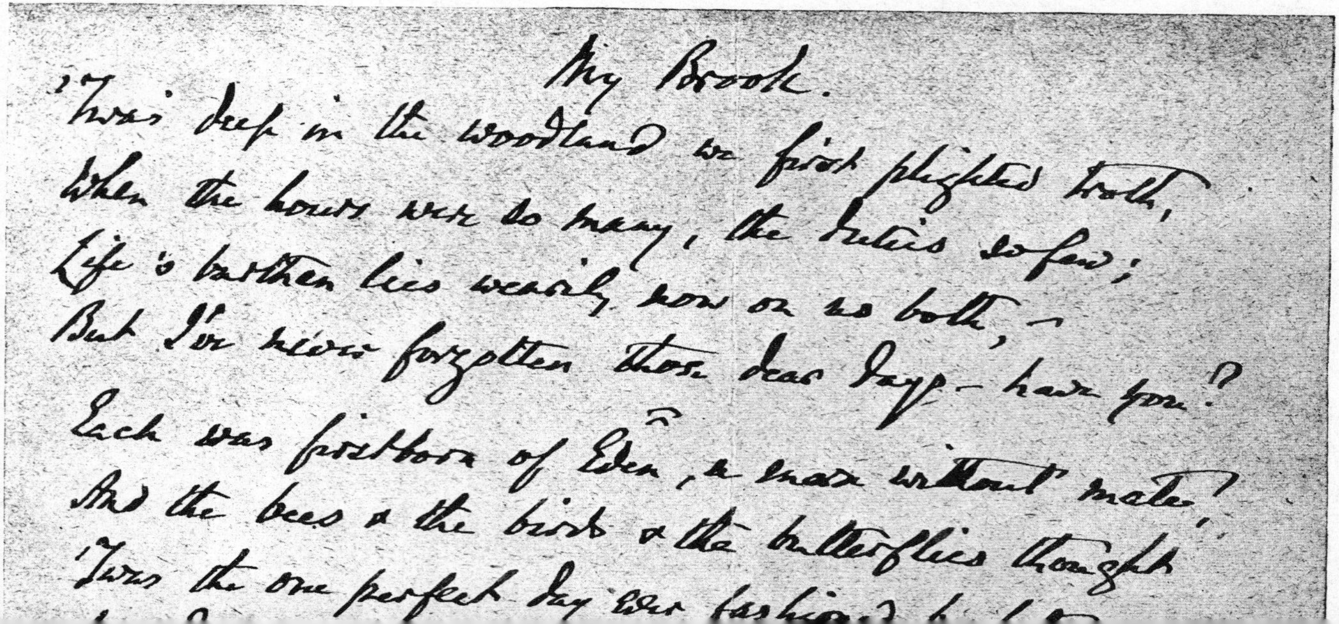

For wearie pilgrims to Dreamland, fair Daughters of Dream,
Which we find again all that we trusted or hoped;
And Fancy, poor fool, with her bauble's supreme.

As the Moors in their style the deep treasured little
Of their Castles in Spain, so to have I, or so feel
That the doors will fly open whenever or while
To the heart of the heart of the Fruit of the year.

14th Sept. 1889.

MY BROOK.[1]

IT was far up the valley we first plighted troth,
   When the hours were so many, the duties so few ;
Earth's burthen weighs wearily now on us both —
   But I 've not forgotten those dear days ; have you ?

Each was first-born of Eden, a morn without mate,
   And the bees and the birds and the butterflies thought
'T was the one perfect day ever fashioned by fate,
   Nor dreamed the sweet wonder for us two was wrought.

I loitered beside you the whole summer long,
   I gave you a life from the waste-flow of mine ;
And whether you babbled or crooned me a song,
   I listened and looked till my pulses ran wine.

'T was but shutting my eyes ; I could see, I could hear,
   How you danced there, my nautch-girl, 'mid flag-root and fern,
While the flashing tomauns tinkled joyous and clear
   On the slim wrists and ankles that flashed in their turn.

———

Ah, that was so long ago !   Ages it seems,
   And, now I return sad with life and its lore,
Will they flee my gray presence, the light-footed dreams,
   And Will-o'-Wisp light me his lantern no more ?

Where the bee's hum seemed noisy once, all was so still,
   And the hermit-thrush nested secure of her lease,
Now whirr the world's millstones and clacks the world's mill —
   No fairy-gold passes, the oracles cease !

The life that I dreamed of was never to be,
   For I with my tribe into bondage was sold ;
And the sungleams and moongleams, your elf-gifts to me,
   The miller transmutes into work-a-day gold.

———

What you mint for the miller will soon melt away ;
   It is earthy, and earthy good only it buys,

But the shekels you tost me are safe from decay ;
   They were coined of the sun and the moment that flies.

Break loose from your thralldom !   'T is only a leap ;
   Your eyes 't is but shutting, just holding your breath ;
Escape to the old days, the days that will keep.
   If there 's peace in the mill-pond, so is there in death.

Leap down to me, down to me !   Be, as you were,
   My nautch-girl, my singer ; again let them glance,
Your tomauns, the sun's largess, that wink and are there,
   And gone again, still keeping time as you dance.

Make haste, or it may be I wander again ;
   It is I, dear, that call you ; Youth beckons with me ;
Come back to us both, for, in breaking your chain,
   You set the old summers and fantasies free.

You are mine and no other's ; with life of my life
   I made you a Naiad, that were but a stream ;
In the moon are brave dreams yet, and chances are rife
   For the passion that ventures its all on a dream.

––––––––

Leapt bravely !   Now down through the meadows we 'll go
   To the Land of Lost Days, whither all the birds wing,
Where the dials move backward and asphodels blow ;
   Come flash your tomauns again, dance again, sing !

Yes, flash them and clash them on ankle and wrist,
   For we 're pilgrims to Dreamland, O Daughter of Dream !
There we find again all that we wasted or misst,
   And Fancy — poor fool ! — with her bauble 's supreme.

As the Moors in their exile the keys treasured still
   Of their castles in Spain, so have I ; and no fear
But the doors will fly open, whenever we will,
   To the prime of the Past and the sweet of the year.

––––––––

And so " my brook " passes into the ocean.

INDEX

INDEX